African Style ✳ *down to the details*

African Style
down to the details

Sharne Algotsson

with Katherine Zoe Andrews

PHOTOGRAPHS BY GEORGE ROSS

 Clarkson Potter/Publishers
New York

Published by Clarkson Potter/Publishers, New York, New York.
Member of the Crown Publishing Group.

Random House, Inc. New York, Toronto, London, Sydney, Auckland
www.randomhouse.com

CLARKSON N. POTTER is a trademark and POTTER and colophon are registered
trademarks of Random House, Inc.

Printed in China

DESIGN BY JANE TREUHAFT

Library of Congress Cataloging-in-Publication Data
Algotsson, Sharne.
    African style : down to the details / Sharne Algotsson.
    1. Ethnic art in interior decoration.   2. Interior decoration—African influ-
    ences.   I. Title.
    NK2115.5.E84 A44 2000
    709'.67—dc21   99-086295

ISBN 0-609-60532-1

10 9 8 7 6 5 4 3 2 1

First Edition

FRONTISPIECE: The rich mud cloth, soft leather, and decorative nail-head trim of this sofa characterize the rugged elegance of African style. Sofa designed by Allen Price, available at Kente Ventures, Inc. OPPOSITE: Acacia trees, thatched dwellings, and the world of wildlife are softly portrayed in the tableware design of Hermes of Paris.
FOLLOWING PAGES: From piping and trims to pillows and bedspreads, fabric has the power to adorn, accessorize, and change the feeling of a room. A simple trim made from an African-printed fabric changes the character of this sheer linen curtain. Tablecloths and bed pillows would be perfect candidates for contrasting trims.

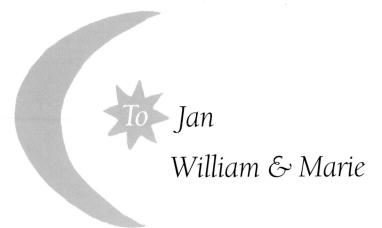

To Jan

William & Marie

"There is always something new out of Africa."

—Pliny the Elder, A.D. 23–79

acknowledgments

Many thanks to my family, Jan, Vanessa, Kay Curtis, Odis Johnson, and Dr. June Powell, for their ever-ready support and encouragement. To my sister-in-law, Valerie Johnson, for producing many of the soft furnishings, and to my friend decorative painter Cheryl Levin, for bringing to life the strikingly colorful walls that I could only imagine.

To the following people I am most grateful for contributing products and services: G. Anthony Fisher and Deborah Cholet, Ahmed and Nandi Tahir, Mel Fisher, Al and Janet Sitnick, Delaware Office of the Urban League, Gloria Leibovitz, Hariette Schiffer, Ignacio Villarrel, Dan Sekanwagi, Liz Galbraith, Ephraim Paul, Epee Ellong, Kwabena Smith, Adeshole Olaniyi, Tihera Amatullah, Aid to Artisans, Ahmad Kenya, and Marion Feltman. Many thanks to the home owners, designers, and artists: Betty and Bill Baumann, Cheryl Campbell and David Teague, Karen Dugger, Gunnel Hasselbach, Mary Ellen and Charles Stadtlander, Nefertiti, Wendy Osterweil, Janet Taylor Pickett, and Dressler Smith.

I would like to extend many thanks to Katherine Zoe Andrews, who worked so attentively on the text, and who brought her creativity as an artist and writer to the manuscript. I would also like to thank Denys Davis, my coauthor of *The Spirit of African Design*, for inviting me to share her dream and inspiring me to take a closer look at African design.

A special thank-you to George Ross, without whose sensitivity for design and love of imagery this book could not have captured the style and beauty of the smallest details, and to his indispensable creative team: Mary Ellen Stadtlander, Lewis Bloom, and Steven Donelian. Additional photographs provided by Gordon Bell courtesy of Mary Engelbreit's *Home Companion,* Bill Baumann, Jacksons 20th-Century Design, Aid to Artisans, Ronnie Johansson, Solvi Dos Santos, Baker Furniture, Kente Ventures, Inc., Houles U.S.A., Takeda Studio, and Lamu Industries.

And to my editor, Annetta Hanna, art director, Marysarah Quinn, and designer, Jane Treuhaft, for their support and guidance.

contents

Color, Paint, *and* Pattern
21

Textiles
65

the spirit. It is about the personal touch that expresses who we are and where we come from.

African style comes to life by incorporating new elements with furnishings we already own and cherish—pieces that possess special meaning and can be enhanced with an attention to decorative details. Most of us have furniture tucked away in attics and basements, pieces that have too much sentimental value to be placed on the curbside. I had one such piece, a small love seat once the pride of my mother's furniture collection. She eventually replaced it with a newer model, and the sofa languished in the basement for almost fifteen years with other forgotten treasures. One day I started looking for just such a small sofa for my own home. I remembered the great lines of that love seat and went browsing in the basement. I couldn't believe it was still there after so many years. The sofa is well made, the style is classic, but its real beauty resides in its sentimental value. To retrieve something that my mother cherished for many years—this is priceless. And to refinish it in African style—what could be better?

I hope this book will answer your design questions and guide you through the process of creating personal interpretations of African style. Then, at the end of the day, when you shut the door on the stresses of the outside world, you will return to a beautiful, tranquil place filled with spirit, a home that cherishes the past down to the very last detail.

Sharne Algotsson

introduction

The Essence of African Style

What is African style and how do you recognize it? These are the questions I encounter most frequently when I give lectures and work with clients. You don't have to be an expert on the subject, but the more you know about Africa, the more easily you will be able to identify African style and incorporate it into your own home. Mother Africa never ceases to surprise me with her overwhelming beauty and diversity. The continent is home to more than fifty nations, and its terrain includes everything from deserts and rain forests to snowcapped mountains. Africa's population spans an exotic range from nomadic tribes that follow their herds' seasonal migration to young professionals who spend their days tracking the stock market. African style seeks to capture this rich complexity. It is not just about incorporating African masks and textiles into pretty interiors. Instead, it goes beyond stereotypes and revives the African tradition of hands-on, do-it-yourself, down-to-the-details design.

There are several hallmarks of African style. First, African style is traditional and modern at the same time. There is a certain timeless, progressive quality to the most ancient of African images. Think of the centuries-old West and Central African masks and figurines that inspired the likes of Matisse and Picasso at the turn of the twentieth century. Or consider the ancient technique of casting gold, cire perdue, perfected in the Ivory and Gold Coasts. Sixteenth-century artisans used images of gold pelicans, elephants, stars, crescents, and gos-

LEFT: Mixing patterns can be tricky, but it can also give you original and striking results. Here Kente and Ewe cloth textiles harmonize through the common denominator of color.

samer wings to create designs that are considered sophisticated and modern even today because of their abstract, graphic style. This rich marriage of the traditional and the modern can also be found in African textiles, masks, sculpture, furniture, and jewelry.

Simplicity is another hallmark. In fact, it is the simplicity of the style that makes it so timeless. Traditionally, Africans rarely decorated for the sake of decoration alone. Instead, they used design and decoration as a kind of visual communication—to express, for example, marital status, religious affiliation, or tribal identity. They chose simple, pared-down images, patterns and textures that could broadcast information clearly. Kuba cloth, a tightly woven raffia appliquéd with geometric designs, is a perfect example of this spare style. Bringing the simplicity of African style to your walls, floors, furniture, windows, and accessories is no easy feat. You'll have to apply some artistic restraint to rein in the universe of rich possibilities.

African style is also spiritual. African culture celebrates the world of the spirit and connects it to everyday life. The continent is replete with rites of worship that feature ceremonial masks and sculptures known for their animated, almost futuristic design. A reverence for ancestors and the forces of nature permeates all forms of African art and goes to the heart of African style.

The final hallmark of African style is its almost chameleon-like flexibility. African style easily blends with and complements other styles. The progressive character of

African design makes it a comfortable fit with contemporary home furnishings. From Morocco to Namibia, Africa's enormous cultural and natural diversity has inspired versatile styles that can accommodate a variety of individual interpretations and lifestyles. You can find a style that will work for you. You might prefer African modern or contemporary African, African Country, Afro-Euro, African rustic, or classical African—the options are endless.

African style doesn't have to scream "Africa!" It can be as improvisational or as traditional as you like. The only rule is that it should always be livable. Between the covers of this book, you will find many suggestions for achieving the essence of Africa in your home—without having to sacrifice the way you live or the things you love. The furnishings you already own and the objects you already treasure are often the perfect place to begin an African revival.

Where to Begin

Answering the following question will launch you on your African revival and put everything into practical perspective: What is your budget? Doing the numbers will help you define the scope of your decorating plan. Remember, bigger is not always better. There are many ways to get more out of every dollar, and a modest budget can be a rewarding creative challenge.

Once you have determined your budget, the fun can begin. How will your home take on the look and feel of Africa? What image are you trying to create? Use some basic rules as your guide. First, discover your own sense of style. Your personal vision of Africa will then be expressed in every nook and cranny of your home. Second, never lose sight of

OPPOSITE: Curvaceous and simple, the form of this Nigerian hand-crafted reptile figure instinctively evokes an aura of Africa within a room setting. THIS PAGE, TOP: Kenyan wood-and-metal spears and Moroccan carved wooden tent stakes. BOTTOM: These contemporary African-inspired fabrics created by an American-based Ugandan designer, Dan Sekanwagi, are perfect for upholstery.

function (in other words, how you really live). When it comes to design, think function first—beauty will follow. Third, be prepared to do it yourself. African-inspired home furnishings can be extremely difficult to find, so be prepared to roll up your sleeves and create your own interpretation of Africa. Fourth, nothing is off limits. Fabric, paint, texture, pattern, furniture, accessories—all are vehicles for expressing your unique response to African style.

The Elements of Decorating in African Style

To decorate in African style, you will need to focus on five design elements: color and paint, patterns and motifs, furniture, textiles, and accessories. These elements are basic to all styles of interior design, but they have their own unique application in African style.

COLOR AND PAINT

Color and paint are key to African style. Color is the heart and soul of Africa, and paint allows us to reproduce any color we wish. Color creates atmosphere, meaning, and identity. The colors we choose for our homes and how we apply them express what and who we are. African-inspired colors run the gamut from neutral earth tones to indigo blues and warm reds. In this book, we will concentrate not just on the primary colors we usually associate with Africa. We will explore a variety of less familiar color schemes that capture the feeling of bright-painted fishing boats at rest on a sandy gold beach, a row of whitewashed bungalows crowned with soft terra-cotta roofs, or the deep blue hues of veils and turbans worn by the Tuareg desert people of Mali and Niger.

PATTERNS AND MOTIFS

Patterns and motifs distinguish African style from other ethnic styles. The sense of spirituality found in African art can be difficult to express in interior design. One way is to use the traditional African symbols that represent timeless proverbs. Ancient in origin, these symbols can become philosophies for the future. The designs are found throughout the continent woven into textile designs, carved into stools, or etched into jewelry. They are graphic and abstract, and express a range of ideas and themes. Of the many ways to bring Africa into the home, the use of African symbols is by far the most unique.

FURNITURE

Furniture requires the most improvisational approach of all the style elements. Nothing is more basic to interior design than choosing just the right furniture. A designer will consider not only style but also material, function, scale, and proportion. Incorporating African elements with the functional pieces we already own is one of the biggest challenges of decorating in African style. For example, the traditional furnishings of West and Central Africa—stools, chairs, ottomans, and other beautifully sculpted pieces—play an important role in the visual impact of a room but are consid-

OPPOSITE, TOP: More than earth colors and primary hues, pastels from creamy soft tones to cool citrus find a place in African style. These colors are great for architectural details, baseboards, and trims. MIDDLE: The Nsoroma star motif and the Sankofa heart-shaped symbol are two of the more familiar Ghanaian Adinkra symbols chosen as stencil patterns. BOTTOM: Look to nature for exciting color combinations and inspiration. THIS PAGE, TOP: Embroidery of the Dwanimen or Ram's horn Adinkra symbol is one of many examples of how we can incorporate pattern and motifs into home decor. MIDDLE: Pattern and motif transforms Richard L. Bryant's contemporary cabinet into a work of art, satisfying both our love of beautiful furniture and our need for everyday function. BOTTOM: An eclectic mix of dark wood, chocolaty leather, sumptuous wool, and vintage metal add to the ambience.

ered accent or occasional furnishings. We need other pieces to satisfy the requirement of our day-to-day activities and contemporary lifestyles. Here we look to what we already own. We can breathe new life into upholstered sofas and chairs, into beds, chests of drawers, and tables using fabric, paint, and accessories.

TEXTILES

Textiles provide the greatest opportunity to make the leap into African-inspired interior design. Craftsmen on the continent have been perfecting techniques of weaving, dyeing, stamping, and appliquéing textiles for centuries, so it is no surprise that the beauty and range of African textiles is unparalleled. Slipcovers, cushions, canopies, fabrics draped across walls, tables, and windows—all add color, texture, and pattern to a room. African textiles are not readily available everywhere. Give yourself plenty of time to find the right fabrics. They can be expensive, but you can keep costs down and introduce interesting visual contrasts by combining African textiles with other fabrics such as velvet, silk, linen, or corduroy. Think about mixing different patterns to create a riot of design. And always consider wall color, furnishings, and the overall mood of the room when selecting fabrics.

ACCESSORIES

Accessories make a room your own. What do you do when your furniture looks great, your walls glow with the perfect color, your window treatments are just right, but something is still missing? That missing element is often the intimate feeling that comes from the little things, the accessories. Framed photographs or letters, fabric samples mounted and arranged on a wall, feather trims and tassels incorporated into a pillow as cover and piping—personal treasures like these can give your home your individual touch. The key here is not really the items in themselves but the detailed attention you pay them. You can make an individual design statement through your choice and arrangement of accessories. When you connect the emotional dots, the sum of the smaller decorating parts will add the finishing touch to your overall design.

Contemporary African design can bring Africa home in a fresh way. Something new is always coming out of Africa. Most of us have come to know African art and design from a traditional perspective. But African style is ever evolving. Hand-carved Ashanti stools, Senufo wash stools, and Masai milking stools are masterpieces of craftsmanship and original design, but so are the works of the craftsmen and designers of the twenty-first century. These new expressions have their roots firmly planted in the traditions of simple sculptural forms, natural materials, and spiritualism. They are the perfect vehicles for creating a contemporary African style in your home.

Today more and more of us are striving to bring personal meaning and beauty into our lives and homes. African style is the perfect way to express that joy in living, whether your look is formal, traditional, minimal, casual country, or eclectic. Small spaces are never too small to be both functional and beautiful, and upscale interiors are a perfect match for the exquisite design and craftsmanship of African art. Some will want to boldly applaud Mother Africa in their interior design; others will want to quietly whisper of the part of the continent that captures their soul. The opportunities are as limitless as your imagination.

OPPOSITE, TOP: Pillows are the perfect way to incorporate color, pattern, and texture into a room. Fabric such as Kuba cloth can singlehandedly make the African connection. MIDDLE: Bowls, trays, flowers, or even food add decorative detailing, and at the same time create a personal connection. BOTTOM: An African-American soldier's Civil War discharge document, now a family treasure, is displayed with other family belongings. THIS PAGE, TOP: Instead of a jewelry box, this Moroccan copper tray is excellent storage for a jewelry collection. BOTTOM: A hand-painted barbershop sign from the Ivory Coast and Liz Galbraith lamp with hand-painted shade set the tone for this bedside table.

Color, *and* Paint, Pattern

Colors shimmer, they glow, they mix and mingle, they create not only their own beauty but the beauty each of us perceives. It is hard to imagine a world without this visual powerhouse that moves us spiritually and emotionally. Color can soothe our hearts, lift our spirits, energize our minds. It can make us feel jubilant or sad, agitated or calm.

As if by magic, color can create the illusion of a new world or evoke some of our most vivid memories. We all have our favorite colors, and favorite colors can ultimately become favorite rooms.

In a style of interior design inspired by Africa, color is crucial. Color runs to the heart and soul of Mother Africa—a place where nature is both cruel and kind, where snowcapped mountains, deserts, and rain forests have dominated the landscape and culture for centuries, and where the very people reflect this natural diversity. The continent's contrasts and combinations are breathtaking, from the lush green towering canopies in the rain forests of West and Central Africa to the spectacular golden sand dunes of the Namib Desert to the deep indigo seas of the fishing villages on the continent's West Coast.

How can you tap into the power of color in your own home? Most designers agree that the easiest and most cost-effective way to change the overall look and feel of a space is through the use of paint. Paint can breathe new life into a room. The colors you choose and where you decide to place them can fundamentally change how you perceive the space around you. You can use paint to raise ceilings, shorten corridors, camouflage architectural defects, or celebrate key features. You can apply light colors to open up a room for a feeling of airy spaciousness or use dark colors to draw in walls for drama and intimacy.

Pattern is another way to introduce color into a room. In fact, the movement of any pattern

PRECEDING PAGES: A dressing table draped in contemporary purple and gold Lurex Asoke textile becomes an island of interest. The contemporary Moroccan table lamp, made of wrought iron, unites color and pattern. Ceramics, jewelry, and perfume bottles all add to the exotic flavor of the interior. The Moroccan lamp and ceramics are from Cob Web and the Asoke is from LSF for Wonoo Ventures, Ltd. THIS PAGE: To contrast with the striking warm hue of the hall walls, the doorway and baseboards were painted in a cool mint green, the shade of this vintage parfait chair.

depends on the interaction of color. Often symbolic in nature, African patterns tell stories and celebrate the spirit. Woven textiles, appliquéd motifs, stamped prints, and batiked and embroidered designs are just a few options from Africa's rich store of powerful patterns. You can create a vibrant feel by trimming window and door frames in Adinkra symbols. You can be bold and design your own African-inspired mural or give old tables and chairs a second life by covering them in traditional African motifs.

Africa will give you endless color options to mull over as you begin the exciting process of decorating your interior. You can choose hues that send you back in time—or create a contemporary feel of Africa.

Color as Inspiration

Africa is a continent of inspiration—just one story can give rise to a host of colors and textures. Timbuktu, the ancient city of commerce and learning, was just such a source of inspiration for me. Located in Mali on the southwest fringes of the Sahara Desert, Timbuktu was the center of Islamic culture and became the crossroads of trans-Saharan trade—mostly in gold and salt—between West Africa and the Muslim world. The city reached the pinnacle of its power and influence during the fourteenth century under the rule of Mansa Musa. This sultan led a legendary pilgrimage from

RIGHT: Hallways are critical spaces in any interior, and color has the power to transform them as much as any other room. Two layers of paint have been applied to this corridor. The first coat of orange was applied to the original white wall, and then thinned out by randomly patting the paint with cheese cloth. The second coat—a mixture of the same orange paint thinned with a little water, raw umber, and a glaze solution—darkened the color a bit and quieted it down. Finally, the walls were treated with a coat of varnish, which added a protective layer and a slightly darker tint.

ABOVE: A Gabbra woman from Moyale, Kenya, embodies the panorama of cultures throughout the African continent. Her silky soft pastel fabrics are a rich contrast to many of the textiles from West and Central Africa, of which we are more familiar. Interpreting African style is all about choosing those exotic aspects that speak to you. LEFT: A collection of colorful accessories atop a contemporary Egyptian wrought-iron and glass table brings out the theme and echoes the vivid color palette of the room. A brass lantern, a Moroccan blue glass, and a bouquet of ranunculuses and delphiniums chime with the organza and silk fabrics. The Egyptian table and brass lantern are from Cob Web. OPPOSITE: Color doesn't have to be overpowering. In this room, vivid primary colors are expressed in a whisper. Purple, orange, red, yellow, and gold coexist harmoniously. The room sets out to capture the exoticism of the legendary city Timbuktu. Invoking tales of trade caravans that slowly crisscrossed the Sahara, the fabrics shimmer like the desert sands—from red to yellow organza to gold Lurex threads to silk and wool rugs. The French wrought-iron chair adds a touch of romance and the wall's Ghanaian Adinkra symbols transport us back to spiritual times.

Timbuktu to the holy city of Mecca. An entourage of some 60,000 people accompanied him on the 1,000-mile journey across the Sahara Desert. With him, Mansa Musa transported tons of gold dust to offer as tokens of goodwill and to pay for services along the way. Thus scattering his gold dust throughout the Middle East, Mansa Musa made Timbuktu famous as a city of untold wealth.

This story drifted through my mind as I flew over the Sahara for more than two hours and looked across the horizon with nothing but peaking sand dunes in sight. Imagine the royal entourage clad in regal red and dark purple protective veils, the coffers of gold shimmering in the desert sun. To me, Timbuktu was a place of romance. So when I set out to create a bedroom inspired by the ancient city, I asked myself, What is the color of romance? The colors I chose were gold, orange, yellow, magenta, and purple. Gold gleams in the embroidered patterns of the bed linens and in the threads of a Nigerian Asoke fabric; sunlight transforms the organza window fabric into a glittering gold hue. The walls combine mint green and orange, applied in a faux finish. The soft, light tones speak of a mysterious world of veils and turbans. Combining pastel colors and intricate geometric designs with indigo and colorful motifs captures the spirit of this cosmopolitan city and its complex Afro-Islamic character.

When choosing an African-style palette for your interior, go with whatever inspires you about Africa's grand panorama of people, places, and things. You might find inspiration in the vivid colors of tropical orchids, water lilies, and amaryllises, or in the orange, black, and yellow of the black-eyed Susan. The rich purple of African violets, creamy beige of raffia, and soft brown of sisal capture the feeling of Africa in more

subtle tones. These kinds of rich color associations will invariably carry over to other design elements, such as pattern and texture, and give your space an emotional vibrancy and coherence.

Traveling to Africa and experiencing it firsthand is a wonderful way to create your own journal of ideas. There's nothing quite

ABOVE: A Gabbra woman of Kenya performs the traditional task of weaving a matrimonial milk container for her daughter. LEFT: Two Massai women are striking in their dramatic flat neck collars made of colorful beadwork wire and earrings and armbands. An interior color scheme can easily be inspired by such imagery. OPPOSITE: The wide variety of clay and glass beads is an excellent inspiration for developing interior decorating color combinations.

like it. You will see Africa's colors not just in broad sunlight but through the filter of a light noon rain. A collection of souvenirs—seashells, postcards, photographs, clothing, jewelry—can be a rich visual resource. Of course, you can find color inspiration closer to home, too. Bookstores are great resources, especially those with travel and design sections. If a photograph in a book or a magazine inspires you, hold on to it. My archive of magazine tear sheets is invaluable to me as a designer. I am always flipping through magazines to update it with whatever new color image catches my eye, and I return to my archive again and again for ideas and inspiration. Another way to spark an idea is by browsing through shops that specialize in African textiles, masks, handcrafts, baskets, or jewelry. A close look at a hand-woven basket made by the Zulu of South Africa or fabric woven by the Ewe of Ghana reveals volumes about how you can mix and apply primary colors in a variety of tonal values.

Using a Color Board

Choosing your color scheme is the most effective way of directing the mood of your interior. When choosing a scheme, don't just think of your walls. Consider every component in the room—upholstered and hard furniture, accent furnishings, window

treatments, artwork, accessories, plants, and flowers. The best way to strike the right balance among your color elements is to construct a storyboard or color board. Use an 11- X 17-inch piece of art board to assemble decorating samples and ideas for your room. Experiment with different combinations of main colors and accents. The more impact a color will have in your room, the more prominently it should figure on your board. You can include color chips, finishes, and samples of wallpaper, fabric, and carpets. If you're thinking about having decorative trim or other embellishments on your furniture or accessories, try to include samples of them as well. And don't forget the souvenirs, photographs, and

tear sheets that have inspired your personal vision of Africa. Developing a storyboard in this way lets you see how your colors will come together *before* you commit to them. Maybe that bright orange you love so much is too overpowering for the walls and would function better as an accent. Better to know before you invest time and money in painting your space.

The most familiar African color scheme is inspired by West African Kente cloth and other strip weaves famous for their vibrant primary colors—red, yellow, green, blue, and black. These luxurious hues summon images of the entire region of West Africa, home to the Gulf of Guinea, the Gold Coast, and the Ivory Coast, as well as Nigeria, Benin, Togo, Liberia, and Sierra Leone. Each area has its own rich history of ceremonial textiles, beaded regalia, clothing, mural painting, and jewelry, all of which are

Family Room Floor Plan

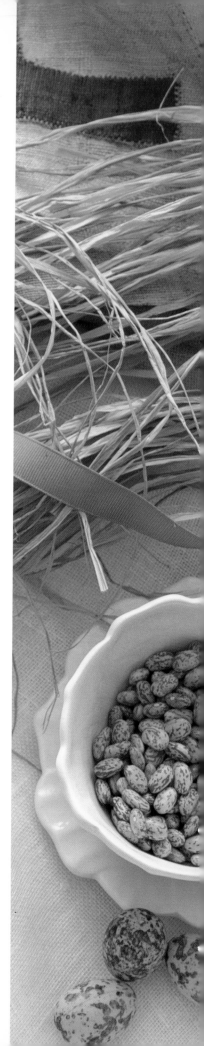

characterized by their explosive colors. These hues have natural sources: West African craftsmen traditionally looked to turmeric, kola nuts, and flowering plants for shades of yellow; guinea corn, henna, and camwood trees for red; mud for black; and indigofera plants for blue. If primary colors don't speak to you, turquoise, terra-cotta, purple, or pastels can just as easily evoke the feeling of West Africa. Don't be afraid to experiment with less familiar color schemes. As long as you allow inspiration to be your guide, the results will be beautiful and distinctively yours.

African style can be as joyful as yellow, as dazzling as red, as mysterious as blue, as tranquil as beige, or as rich as brown. Color is a key visual stimulant, and different colors create very different moods.

neutral colors

Neutral and soft natural colors, also referred to as earth tones, radiate relaxation and calm. Monochromatic schemes include colors such as alabaster, ivory, bone, beige, sepia, taupe, gray, sage green, and mustard, and each of these hues contains an inexhaustible range of subtle gradations. Neutral color schemes can give any space a sensual feel. The colors glow warmly in the sunlight and invite the touch by picking up the interplay of light and shadow in a way that accentuates the contrasts of textures in fabrics and finishes. Mono-

RIGHT: Clean and simple, muted and monochromatic, neutrals make a perfect backdrop for all things African and focus the eye on contrasting textures. Assembled here, clockwise from top, are a woven raffia cloth with embroidered patterns, covered with raffia in its original form; a contemporary upholstery fabric in a cream and beige geometric pattern; necklaces made from polished amber beads, pieces of ostrich eggs and silver, birds' eggs, and pinto beads, all in subtle neutral tones. Contemporary upholstery fabrics are produced by Arte Wall Covering and Fabrics, Inc.

LEFT: The lighter and softer look of West Africa, as expressed in this bedroom, includes white waffle weave cotton and silky Adinkra patterns embroidered on heavy linen. Nigerian Asoke textile, now a wall hanging, and the Dogon and Ashanti stools from Mali and Ghana strike a balance of earth tones. When mixing and layering accessories, remember that natural fabrics, wood finishes, and other organic materials create not only tactile pleasure but emotional warmth as well. Let earth colors and natural organic textures direct your choice of accessories and accents. RIGHT: The calla lily, also known as the trumpet lily and pig lily, is indigenous to Africa and grows wild in fields and on the banks of streams and rivers in South Africa. Such flowers are the perfect accessory for African-style interiors. BELOW: These baskets, although not African inspired, can be added to the mix. Their earth coloring, textured surfaces, and geometric forms complement all things African. The baskets are available at The Menagerie, Ltd.

neutral colors

chromatic walls are the perfect backdrop for artwork, lamps, figurines, and other accessories. Neutral color schemes are commonly associated with uncluttered modern interiors, but creamy soft hues can be the perfect choice for cozy traditional spaces as well.

RIGHT: The color of nightfall and calm seas, blue can be dramatic and tranquil. A popular color choice, blue changes from warm to cool, depending on the accompanying colors. Incorporate shades of blue into your home with flowers, fabric, ceramics, glass, and tableware. From top, clockwise, an intricate batik cloth created by Nigerian textile artist Adeshola Olaniyi; a decorative platter; voluminous beaded necklaces from the Ivory Coast; indigo cloths; and Moroccan glass. The batik cloth is available from LFS for Wonoo Ventures, Ltd.; the platter is from Bamboula, Ltd.; the necklaces are from Craft Caravan; the indigo cloths are available at A & J Fabrics; and the glass is from Cob Web.

blues

We all know what it means to have the blues, but blue can also be as uplifting as the azure heavens or as mysterious as the deep sea. It can be calming, soulful, thoughtful. Blue color schemes are favorites of many decorators. For instance, combinations of vibrant blues with white and yellow are central to traditional Scandinavian and French interior design.

African-style design often emphasizes a luxuriously deep blue. Indigo is one of the most loved blues of Africa. An organic dye made from the indigofera plant, indigo can range from soft, light shades to rich, blue-black tones. Indigo dye originated in ancient Egypt, where deep blue fabrics were produced before the birth of Christ.

The African center of indigo dyeing is the Nigerian city of Kano, where fabrics are produced in varying shades. To the north in Mali, Mauritania, and Niger, Tuareg women prize Kano-made cloth and fashion the soft blue fabrics into gowns. Tuareg men traditionally drape themselves in turbans and veils of the darkest indigo to protect themselves from harsh desert winds. Because the indigo cloth tends to shed its metallic dye and settle on the face, they are known as the blue men of the desert.

A blue color scheme gives you a lot of flexibility. A deep, nearly black indigo makes a strong, dramatic statement. A color with this kind of impact can close in an already small

LEFT: Some consider deep blue to be too exciting a color for a place of slumber. That is not the case here. Blue lends this bedroom a dramatic serenity. The bold patterns and organic textures of natural fabrics, wood, wrought iron, rope, and sisal combine to create an earthy but sumptuous room. The bed linens are from IKEA; the blanket is from Bamboula, Ltd. RIGHT: The agapanthus, also known as lily of the Nile, comes from Africa. Its graceful stems and delicate lilac-colored flowers are great as cut flowers or a house plant. Flowers are a terrific way to bring out existing colors in a fabric. BELOW: Add color even in the smallest details. Glass buttons, beads, and other small details are just one way to make the color connection. Use them to adorn place mats, pillows, slipcovers, and the like.

blues

space, but it is just the thing if you are thinking of creating a feeling of cozy intimacy instead of the illusion of spaciousness. Darker shades of blue mix well with accents of orange, gold, pink, purple, and beige on doors, window frames, or architectural features.

To create an airy feeling in your space, choose pastel blues such as aqua and turquoise and combine them with pastel pinks, terra-cottas, and yellows. You can use such combinations to mimic the intricate tile floors and mosaic tabletops of North Africa.

yellows

Cheerful, bright, and airy, yellow has the power to lift the spirits. The warm glow of afternoon sunshine or a bouquet of bright sunflowers radiates cheer. Shades of yellow range from ocher, a warm earth tone with traces of brown or orange, to crisp lemon yellow. Yellow enhances the organic and natural quality of African art. It is an integral element of Africa's parched tundra where camels are the preferred means of transportation and cattle are prized possessions. People of the Sudan, Kenya, Somalia, Ethiopia, Tanzania, and Uganda move in a migratory pattern, packing up their homes and families five or six times a year in search of more abundant vegetation and game. You can use yellow to conjure up this arid desert landscape, especially when you apply it as a faux finish, layering a bright wash over a darker hue.

LEFT: Cheerful and lively, yellow captures the sunny vitality and pulsating excitement of Africa. This ensemble consists of colorful silk handwoven Kente cloth, Central- and West African–inspired upholstery fabrics produced by Arte Wallcovering and Fabrics, Inc., and yellow and orange fruit and flowers. Remember to look to the natural world when it comes to color.
RIGHT: The cheerful nature of yellow and the whimsical look of sunflowers make these flowers a light-hearted choice when introducing yellow.

yellows

RIGHT: Architectural detailing often found in older homes—deep windowsills, built-in bookcases, fireplace mantels, and paneled wainscoting—offer opportunities to incorporate accent color in dramatic ways. This built-in cabinet provides an exciting frame for glass, tableware, and other dining accessories. BELOW RIGHT: The crisp, cool tone of lemon yellow is perfect for more contemporary African interiors. BELOW LEFT: The elaborate mud-cloth tapestry from Mali was made with earth colors and mud textures. OPPOSITE: With walls of yellow ocher and afternoon west lighting, this room is awash in a cheerful yellow glow. This hue is reflected in the tactile surfaces and monochromatic colors of the straw, sea grass, and sisal furnishings.

browns

Often considered drab or dull, brown is the most underappreciated color in interior decorating. Many pass it over for more familiar hues without properly investigating the wide spectrum of tones available. Red-browns, blue-browns, chocolate browns—all are deep, dark, and delicious. Brown is the color of silky fur, soft suede, and buttery leather. The color exudes sophistication, mystery, and an earthy richness. It just takes a bit of imagination and daring to try a soft terracotta or a deep coffee.

A brown color scheme can complement tropical woods such as rosewood, teak, mahogany, African walnut, or ebony. And it is the perfect backdrop for black-and-white photographs, tropical flowers, and raffia textiles. Barkcloth, a red-brown fiber peeled from the trunks of fig trees, can serve as a unifying motif for a range of earth tones. Natural hardwood floors in varying shades of brown possess a warm beauty that carpet or vinyl simply cannot match. Brown mixes easily with almost any other color, especially pastels such as pink, baby blue, lilac, and green.

LEFT: Rich brown tones vary from the simple to the sophisticated. Resting on traditional bark cloth, a variety of textures—rough glass, smooth amber, and polished bone beads, ranging in colors from terra-cotta to cocoa—creates an interesting mix. At top left, traditional Zairian Showa mats with embroidered geometric symbols contrast with contemporary upholstery print fabrics, directly below, which are designed and produced by U.S.-based Ugandan textile designer Dan Sekanwagi for Visual Feast Fabrics. At bottom center, "Ashanti, Tanala," produced by Arte Wallcovering and Fabrics, Inc., offers options for covering chairs, sofas, even windows in the spirit of Africa. At bottom right, Raffia-woven Kuba cloth, enhanced with appliquéd geometric symbols, and, above, a women's cloth from Gambia, made of rich brown cotton and silver threads, are two other African textiles to consider when decorating your interiors in brown tones.

browns

ABOVE: Subtle detailing and an elegantly carved patterned border embellish a cherry wood mirror. This is designed by Richard L. Bryant for International Design Group, available from Kente Ventures, Inc. OPPOSITE: Ocher yellow walls, rich dark wood, accessories in contrasting colors, and lush leafy green plants create an earthbound beauty that is the hallmark of African style. All of the furnishings here have been given a second life with new upholstery, cushions, and pillows. The contemporary pastel collage on paper by African-American artist Janet Taylor Pickett is at the center; it shares the limelight with a six-foot ceremonial mask from Burkina Faso. The mask is from Findings.

LEFT: Fiery shades of red can set a room aglow, its walls becoming a dazzling backdrop for artwork and furnishings. Reds ranging from dusty pink to tomato can also radiate the softer spirit of nature. An intense orange wall paint was toned down a bit by adding a layer of burnt umber. RIGHT: Vibrant, exciting, dynamic, the color red has a prominent place in ceremonial art and symbolic design throughout Africa. Each culture imbues the hue with its own meaning. For example, in Madagascar, it is associated with burials and mourning, with red shrouds used to cover the dead. In Nigeria, by contrast, red is considered the color of success and luxury. Clockwise from top right: A soft "George," an Indian fabric export to Nigeria; an East-African cotton cloth; and a Sudanese cotton fabric. Painted enamel over tin bowls hail from Niger, and a covered woven basket from Kenya holds an abundance of Tamba beads from the Ivory Coast.

reds

Here is a color that grabs your attention. Red can be quite intimidating. Think about it: When was the last time you saw a red upholstered sofa, painted a red wall, or purchased a red carpet? But red is a versatile hue. It is not just the color of fire engines but also the velvety hue of roses or the pale tone of early tomatoes. And red holds a special place in the world of African art and culture. In Nigeria, for example, red is a symbol of success and achievement; in Madagascar it is the color of burial cloths. In body adornment, royal regalia, garments, jewelry, and textiles, the color evokes the spirit of Africa and its people. It adds a quality of richness to any space when used as an accent color for trims, piping, and borders. Red is a color of choice for African style.

reds

LEFT: Ghanaian Kente cloth makes the perfect bedspread. Woven into strips that are then sewn together, Kente cloth comes in pieces large enough for queen- and king-size beds. This royal blue and orange combination is very popular and sometimes difficult to find. The colorful padded cornice and the trimmed linen curtains make a connection to all the bed linens. TOP: Brilliant colors, whether natural or man-made, seem to be part of the African landscape. From cars and clothes to tropical vegetation, the visual impact of color in everyday life is quite exciting.
ABOVE: Tropical plants, such as Heliconia (also known as the "lobster claw"), can be combined with plants from Africa, such as the bird of paradise, to add additional color, texture, and form to an African interior design.

Painting Techniques

Several years ago I had a vision of a dark blue color scheme for a dining room I was repainting. I had seen a beautiful room with indigo blue walls in a magazine and decided to go with a similar blue. I selected two different paints, but I wasn't satisfied —neither was deep enough. After a closer look at the photograph, I noticed a subtle gradation and shadowing in the paint application and realized that I was looking at not one but two or three overlapping layers of paint. Since gaining that insight, I have abandoned the single-coat paint technique.

Several decorative paint techniques that have become popular over the past few years give the illusion of depth to surfaces. Color washing, glazing, and varnishing are not just techniques for professionals. Don't be afraid to experiment with color. Plan well by doing some research and knowing the precise color you want to achieve before you actually start to paint. Consider color washing, for example. This multilayer technique is a dramatic way to re-create the imagery of Africa in your home with effects as subtle as a cloud or as powerful as a ceremonial ritual. Color washing is actually quite simple. Apply two coats of the color you have chosen to be the dominant tone of your finished wall. Either water-based latex or oil paint will work well. Then let the first two coats dry overnight. Now you are ready for the second layer of color—a combination of pigment and water brushed, sponged, or ragged over the dominant hue. The transparent overlay will add saturation, texture, and depth to your walls.

The Power of Pattern

While window-shopping one afternoon, my cousin and I came across a wonderful sofa displayed in a very fashionable furniture gallery. My cousin was impressed with the combination of pillows covered in a variety of patterns tossed across the sofa. She said with surprise, "I didn't know you could mix so many patterns together, and it could look so good." In fact, it looked great. Just as most people tend to stick with safe, understated colors, so too they shy away from experimenting with pattern in their interior design, afraid that they might overdo it. Don't be afraid—play with different combinations of patterns, motifs, and symbols to create your own mutilayered evoca-

LEFT: The chevrons, stripes, and checkerboard patterns of this mask from Burkina Faso are a powerful spiritual expression of African style. Integrate such bold designs into your interior by using complementary fabric or paint on furniture and walls. This mask is from Findings. BELOW: Circles, Xs, and angled waves convey ritual messages important to the ceremony for which the mask is intended. Bold but simple graphic forms combined with subtle color make this butterfly mask not only a spiritual symbol but also a focal point for an African-inspired interior. The mask is from Indigo Arts.

tion of Africa. You'll be as surprised as my cousin was at how beautiful these diverse arrangements can be.

Pattern brings life to accessories, furniture, walls, and floors. An arrangement of shapes and form can become a kind of visual music whose rhythm and movement define and create moods ranging from mystery and adventure to romance and whimsy.

The dynamic and graphic character of African patterns, motifs, and symbols comprise a virtual treasure trove of decorative possibilities, but they were not created for the purposes of decoration alone. Each pattern—checkerboards, dots, bull's-eyes, strips, chevrons, stylized flowers—has a message and meaning of its own. For example, the checkerboard symbolizes the separation of good and evil, male and female, and is found in Bwa and Nuni masks of Burkina Faso; chevrons represent rivers and mountains that Xhosa painters so vividly depicted; dots symbolize fertility in West Africa; and flowers arranged in kaleidoscopic layout represent a connection to the earth.

ABOVE: A closer look at Ghanaian Adinkra cloth. This cotton fabric stamped with designs was traditionally used for funerals. Embroidered red, yellow, blue, and green threads provide color. Available at LSF for Wonoo Ventures, Ltd. RIGHT: West African style serves up color and pattern in lively and cheerful combinations, but the look is never heavy. The introduction of white into the color scheme of fabrics softens the impact of reds, yellows, and blues. Ghanaian Adinkra cloths large enough to cover a queen-size bed have been transformed into a bedspread. Accessories are kept to a minimum but the look is unmistakably African. Wendy Osterweil's linocut "Seeking Revenge" graces the fireplace. Bed and night table available at IKEA.

CELEBRATING THE SPIRIT

The representational meaning and ritual significance of patterns, motifs, and symbols are essential expressions of the beliefs and philosophies of Africans. The continent's wide range of styles and designs—from the bold and brightly hued geometric, almost digital, patterns of the Ndebele's wall murals to the intricate floral-type designs that characterize Berber carpets and tiles—sets Africa apart from other regions of the world. Over the centuries, nations, ethnic groups, and subgroups have developed and refined their own artistic styles, technologies, and applications. In so doing, Africans have recorded history and provided insight into the future.

Often taking the place of written language, the designs are a kind of visual communication, a medium where verbal and visual meanings come together to offer spiritual or physical protection, interpret omens, or offer blessings. The patterns and symbols depict leadership and tribal affiliation. They represent proverbs and religious principles. Some designs are reserved for men, others for women. Some identify royalty, others specific occupations. In regions of Ghana, the butterfly is a symbol of the wisdom of the chief, while in Burkina Faso, where butterflies appear just before rainfall, butterfly masks are central to rituals celebrating the beginning of the farming season. Images of scarabs and beetles dating back to the early Egyptians symbolize light and knowledge. African proverbs, in both verbal and visual form, are filled with lions, reptiles, snails, fish, chameleons, spiders, tortoises, and antelopes. Every design woven into Kente cloth has a meaning: the Nine Tufts of Hair, for instance, denotes loyalty and a sense of duty; the Apremuo design represents defiance and resistance to colonialism.

The Asante Adinkra symbols are the best known of all African symbols. Dating back to the seventeenth century, Adinkra symbols originally adorned funeral cloths. The Asante people imprinted cotton fabric with a black liquid the consistency of coal tar and stamped motifs onto the fabric using carved pieces of calabash. Artists chose symbols that embodied the qualities of the deceased. A number were repeated across the cloth and together constituted a farewell tribute. Favored today for their clean lines and simple, graphic forms, Adinkra symbols grace exteriors of modern buildings and even contemporary furnishing. Some are universal, such as Osrane ne nsoroma, the star and crescent moon familiar throughout the Arab world, which symbolizes faithfulness. But most are unique, such as Dwenini Mmen, the ram's horns (symbolizing strength), which, because of its beautifully scrolled design, is widely used by designers.

APPLYING PATTERN

There are limitless possibilities for bringing African patterns, symbols, and motifs to interiors. Because of their graphic style, African motifs and symbols are simple enough to embroider or appliqué on pillows, bed linen, tablecloths, napkins, towels, and cushions. And with stencils and paint, you can cover your walls, floors, windows, door frames, and furniture with these powerful symbols. Consider the intensity of your colors when applying patterns to large spaces such as walls and floors. Softer tones will give your patterns a lighter feel. Also, be sensitive to the function of the room you are planning to paint: simple patterns in tranquil colors are just right for a bedroom; let your imagination run wild in larger living spaces and apply big, bold symbols in a range of dramatic colors.

Color is key when combining patterns, motifs, and symbols. It can easily alter the impact of designs. Color or a combination of colors determines whether a single pattern or a collection of patterns becomes the focus of the room. If you are after a soft and tranquil look, express your African rhythms in lighter tones—neutral colors or earthy hues. Kuba designs, for example, have a subdued and discreet beauty. Blues and greens also have a calming quality. For a more dramatic look, choose warm primary colors like the lively reds, yellows, and oranges of Asafo flags. Also, remember to take background colors into account. For example, white backgrounds will lessen the impact of primary colors, particularly red, whereas black will increase their intensity. Strong and graphic patterns make a good marriage with more delicate patterns or those that are dominated by a uniform background color. Be mindful of introducing too many large-scale patterns or motifs: they will dominate the room and vie for attention. Instead mix smaller or continuous patterns—such as woven Kuba, Ewe, Adire, or Kente cloths—with Asafo motifs or other large symbols.

Mixing diverse designs by layering pattern on pattern can yield unpredictable results—sometimes it works instantly; at other times more refining is required. If, however, you trust your taste and never stray from the patterns that speak to your heart, you can't go wrong. Remember, interior decorating is all about expressing who we are and what we like. If you have a minimalist design sensibility, focus on one large pattern painted on canvas or the symmetry of two large pillows covered with a bold graphic design at either end of a sofa. If you like bolder combinations, transform your interior into a playground. Have fun with walls, floors, furniture, lamps, carpets, and small accessories. The rules of combining patterns vary little from one decorating style to another. But the rich diversity of patterns, symbols, and motifs is unique to Africa and African style. The aesthetic options are endless.

Color is magical. It surrounds us with romance, cheer, mystery, and warmth. Africa has been abundantly blessed with a natural and cultural bounty, and color can help you capture it in your own home. Rich ocher walls, dark mahogany furniture, or shimmering organza—the soul of a home is always reflected in color.

OPPOSITE: When choosing furnishings, consider not only their individual characteristics, but how they will coordinate with your accessories and other furnishings. Here, the colors and textures of a sisal rug, woven basket, and curved table leg together express the spirit of African style.

before

A simple, everyday piece of furniture like this table is the perfect place to begin your African revival. You can come up with your own creative interpretations of color and pattern to give your interior that personal touch. Here I lightly sanded the wooden surface until it was smooth. Then I washed the surface with a sponge and soapy water to remove any dirt and residue. I traced the surface to be painted onto a sheet of paper and worked out my design and color scheme before I transferred it in paint to the table.

after

Adinkra
Stenciled Patterns

Age-old African folk patterns have charted the course of lives for generations—they are much more than decoration for the sake of decoration. Some refer to ancient battles; others represent words of wisdom in visual form. Take, for example, the symbol of the crossed reptiles, which symbolizes the need for unity, particularly when there is common destiny.

Two Adinkra patterns in the form of a heart and a star adorn this bedroom wall. The Sankofa heart represents reverence for the past, and the Nsoroma star symbolizes patience and faithfulness. The repetition of the symbols gives the room a real presence, and the fertility dot is the perfect thread to join the two symbols, both thematically and visually. The overall pattern creates a soothing ambience of tranquil spirituality and shimmering brightness. The contrasts of finish and color here are striking: the symbols' glossy and matte paint placed against the textured faux-finished walls, the gold leaf edging up to the soft mint green.

Materials

Clear acetate	Level
Masking tape	Paint
Pencil	Containers for mixing
Surface to cut on	
X-Acto knife	Artist's brush
Tape measure	

Creating the Motifs

1. Choose your design and make sure it is drawn to actual size. A small design can be accurately enlarged on a copy machine.
2. Tape the clear acetate securely over the design so that nothing shifts.
3. Trace the motif with a pencil onto the acetate. For this image you will need to make a second stencil for the coil inside the heart.
4. Place the acetate on a cutting surface, and with the X-Acto knife, cut out the design, leaving short areas of the acetate uncut to hold the stencil together. These areas can be filled in later with paint.
5. Now you are ready to apply the stenciled design to the wall surface.

Painting the Motifs

1. Using the tape measure and level, turn your wall into a grid. Measure each wall, the width of your motifs, and your desired spacing so that the motifs will fit evenly across your walls. With your pencil, mark the spaces between the motifs along the horizontal length of the walls. Repeat this process along the vertical lengths. You will end up with a checkerboard grid.
2. Tape the acetate to the first location you have indicated on the wall.
3. Making sure that the flat artist's brush is drip-free, almost dry, dab paint into the stencil's open spaces.
4. Let the paint set for 30 seconds.
5. Remove the stencil by peeling from top to bottom.
6. Repeat steps 2 through 5 as necessary.

Textiles

Fabric has a way of rounding off the rough edges of a room, and African-inspired interiors are blessed with a rich legacy of limitless textile possibilities.

Africa has long been known for the unparalleled craftsmanship and imagination of its textile artisans.

The time and skill that go into producing just one cloth is astounding —theirs is truly a labor of love.

Consider the story of seventeenth-century Ghanaian and Nigerian weavers encountering silk fabric for the first time. Awed by the look and feel of the unique textile imported from Europe and the Middle East, the weavers sought to reproduce it. The continent had no domesticated silkworms, but the artisans were resourceful. They would unravel the imported silk, dye the threads in new shades, and weave their own textiles out of the recycled material. Today, even in the face of competitive international markets, Africa's ancient textile traditions continue to thrive. The care and craftsmanship that go into producing the fabrics make for beautiful designs that are distinctly African.

The Fabrics of Africa

Many regions of Africa are known for their own particular style of textile design and manufacturing techniques. In the Nigerian city of Ilorin, for example, Yoruba weavers produce a spectacular array of textiles and cloths. One such fabric is called Asoke, a cloth woven of machine-spun cotton with gold Lurex threads interwoven into the openwork strip weave. Traditionally produced for funerals and other religious occasions, Asoke

PREVIOUS PAGES AND RIGHT: When selecting fabrics for an interior, it is important to sample and experiment with different combinations. African textiles mix freely with a variety of fabrics due primarily to the diversity of materials, weaving traditions, and motifs. Colors and patterns that you would have never considered placing together often create original and exotic looks. Here, silk and organza blend with contemporary lilac and gold Nigerian Asoke.

textiles are now exported for decorative use. The openwork weaving technique and gold threads add a touch of elegance to the textiles, making them the perfect choice for draping over a table or hanging on a wall. Remember to keep food and liquids well away from them, however, because the natural fibers absorb stains easily. Since they have a sturdy weave, Asoke fabrics are also just the thing for upholstering sofa pillows and cushions. As with any other strip weave, reinforce the seams using a sewing machine so that they will not separate with repeated use.

Indigo-dyed cloth—produced by the Baule of the Ivory Coast, the Soninke of Senegal, the Yoruba of Abeokuta, and the Hausa of northern Nigeria—is another famous African textile. Hausa dyers are known particularly for producing a very shiny, almost black indigo cloth. The artisans color the cloth using a dry process: they beat the dye into the cloth until it shines. Another indigo textile is resist-dyed Adire cloth with stenciled and batiked patterns. These lightweight cottons are great for window treatments, wall hangings, tablecloths, coverlets, and quilts. Make sure the fabrics are washed several times before using, and always wash them in cold water.

Ghanaian Kente cloth is, for many, the essence of African textile design. Originally woven for Asante royalty in the city of Bonwire, these fabrics are renowned for their high level of craftsmanship, their vibrant primary colors, and their symbolic patterns and motifs. Kentes make wonderful bedspreads or duvets. These high-quality strip-weave fabrics should be dry-cleaned only.

ABOVE: The glitter of Lurex threads and an open-work weaving technique give a distinctive character to these contemporary Asoke textiles produced by the Yoruba of Nigeria. Eclectic colors and patterns mesh well with formal or traditional African-style interiors. The textiles are from Beads of Paradise. OPPOSITE: The wearing of silk Kente cloth was once reserved for the Asantehene, king of the Asante kingdom, and members of the royal court. Today, however, Kente is part of the national costume of Ghana and is produced primarily in cotton and rayon. Recognized for its lavish colors and weaves, which total more than 300 different patterns, Kente is worn for special social and ritual occasions. When selecting these cloths for upholstery, remember to chose the right weight and have the fabric reinforced along the selvage for greater durability. The textiles are from Kente Ventures, Inc.

OPPOSITE: Each of the indigo textiles varies in manufacturing technique. Clockwise from top: A Nigerian Adire resist-dyed fabric with freehand design, an Adire with a stenciled pattern, an indigo tie-dyed cloth, and a Ghanaian strip weave textile with indigo-dyed threads. Adire textiles are from Beads of Paradise and Indigo Arts. ABOVE: Contemporary indigo cloths from Nigeria and colorful mud cloths from Mali may be too heavy for bed pillows but are perfect when used as throws, pillow shams, and seat covers.

ABOVE: Raffia-woven textiles from Zaire express Africa through their minimalist designs. Incorporating pillows covered in traditional fabrics into an interior is an easy way to create the feeling of Africa. The Showa textile that covers the pillow in the foreground is produced in a two-part process of weaving raffia, then adorning it with cut pile embroidery. The large Kuba cloth pillow uses a different weaving technique and is decorated with appliquéd motifs. Textiles are from Indigo Arts.

LEFT: Ewe cloth has two distinctive styles. A more refined version, made of silk, rayon, and high-quality cotton, has inlaid motifs and patterns. This type can be considered a work of art. The other, shown here, is more basic in design and considerably less expensive. However, the ocher, sage green, berry, mustard, burnt sienna, and maroons of this second style all blend wonderfully with contemporary color schemes. The Ewe cloth is from Indigo Arts.

The Ewe of southeastern Ghana make another style of strip-weave textile called Ewe cloth, characterized by more abstract symbols and shapes. There are two types of Ewe cloth—the more expensive woven from silk, the less expensive made of cotton. Ewe colors—subtle reds and oranges, lime greens, maroons, sage greens, and pale yellows—are more muted than Kente hues. If your look is on the soft side of colorful, Ewe cloths are perfect for upholstering sofas or covering standing screens.

African artisans weave raffia, a fiber made of palm leaves, into long textile panels, which were traditionally fashioned into dance skirts for funerals. The Kuba and the Showa have become famous for their abstract designs. Henri Matisse, born into a family of weavers, relished textile design, included Showa mats among his personal collection, and sought inspiration in the geometric designs for his paintings. The Kuba produce highly original designs out of raffia, and their work is quickly becoming the most sought-after African textile in today's interior design market. The subtle neutral color schemes and the minimalist geometric forms of Kuba designs help explain their newfound popularity. The Showa weave another style of raffia textile. The colors tend more toward browns, yellows, and blacks, and the Showa add embroidery and velvety cut pile to the raffia. Both of these unusual textiles are well suited for making pillows, upholstering furniture, or hanging as art. They are the perfect way to incorporate a contemporary feel with a rustic sensibility.

Appliqué motifs are another patterned technique of textile design, created by over-lapping fabric. The results can be striking, particularly in the case of the vibrant banners, flags, and state umbrellas designed and produced by the Fon of Benin and the Fante of Ghana. The one-dimensional appliquéd images of people, animals, and weapons are at once lively and complex. The banners of the Fon illustrate the genealogy of kings who reigned in the land that was once known as Dahomey. Commissioned by military men to chronicle historical events and document their own involvement in battles, the Asafo banners and flags, also produced by the Fon, depict the battles and other life-and-death confrontations of the colonial period. Although the message of these banners is quite serious, they have a light, almost exuberant quality in their subtle animal motifs (crabs, fish, porcupines, and monkeys) and color combinations ranging from red, white, blue, and black to pink, yellow, and red. They continue to be produced today and are documented beautifully by Peter Adler and Nicholas Barnard in *Asafo! African Flags of the Fante*. In the home, these banners and flags instantly convey an attention to beauty and a reverence for history. Large ones can be displayed as wall hangings, narrow ones can function as table runners, and squares can be thrown over the backs of easy chairs.

Contemporary textiles, such as Nigerian George and lace, came to Africa via India and Europe, respectively. George, as it is called in West Africa, has become an essential fabric in Nigerian women's fashion. Used as wraps, shawls, and sashes for beautiful gowns, this silky soft textile is also a great accent fabric for home decor. George is adorned with gold Lurex threads and comes in a variety of attention-grabbing colors such as purple, orange, blue, and red. The fabric is heavily embellished with pearls, sequins, and embroidered patterns. George makes for flamboyant window valances or pillowcases. It is just the thing if you want an outspoken declaration of African style. Nigerian lace, a sheer fabric with elaborate gold-thread embroidery, brings a whimsical feel to an otherwise traditional fabric. The lace functions beautifully as a sheer curtain, soft pillow sham, or elaborate bed ruffle.

ABOVE: A touch of whimsy and the element of surprise are what make this padded window cornice, covered in George, a focal point of this bedroom. RIGHT: Variations of the show-stopping fabric known as George come in a bevy of colors and are adorned with pearls, beads, sequins, and metallic threads. The material is actually produced in India but bears a likeness to the shimmering and glamorous textiles long produced in Nigeria. Among Nigerian women, George is a favorite, used as wraps, sashes, or embellishments for their gowns. George is available at A & J Fabrics.

LEFT: The color, pattern, and texture of different accessories define the look of this room. The purple unites an unexpected cultural mix of accessories: masks and stools, curtains of raw silk, an antique wrought-iron bed frame, pearl-studded window cornices, a duvet trimmed in Indian George, a pillow sham made of Nigerian Asoke, and a Ghanaian strip weave used as a throw. The African textiles are available at LSF for Wonoo Ventures, Ltd. ABOVE: This combination of gold, purple, tangerine, and white whispers Africa. Consider such colors to project the eclectic glamour of African style.

African Fabric at Home

Two questions are essential to consider when choosing African textiles for your home. First, do you want to cut such beautiful—and often expensive—fabrics and turn them into yardage? Strip weaves such as Kente, Asoke, and Ewe cloths are among the most valuable of all African textiles. They are works of art in themselves. If you turn them into upholstery fabric, their life span will be limited. As wall hangings or bedspreads, they will undergo far less wear and tear and will be more likely to endure through the years. Second, are you looking for authentic or African-inspired fabric? A number of companies are beginning to produce African-inspired upholstery fabrics. While they can be relatively expensive, the advantage is that they are treated for stain resistance and they are durable—upholstery products are designed to hold up under stress.

UPHOLSTERY FABRIC

When shopping for upholstery fabric, plan to spend a considerable amount of time visiting fabric stores, boutiques, and specialty stores. Design centers are important resources as well. Although they usually sell only to the industry, most are open to the public on special days. Always take your color samples with you, as well as pillows or throws that show your existing fabrics, to make sure the fabrics that appeal to you will work with your color scheme. Once you have decided on several fabrics, bring samples home and live with them for a few days before you make a final decision. You will avoid any unpleasant surprises in the future by viewing the fabric under a variety of conditions—in broad daylight, at dusk, by candlelight. If you are opting for any of the expensive strip weaves, look for textiles that have holes or any other kind of minor damage. It will be easier and less expensive to turn them into yardage. Moderately priced African textiles such as mud cloth, heavy-gauge indigo cloth, and Ewe cloth are other good upholstery options.

OPPOSITE: Striking a romantic note, these fabrics capture a sense of North Africa, summoning up the turbans and veils worn in desert climes. The silk melds harmoniously with the sheer organza fabric of the window treatment. Light-weight organza is perfect for draping, and its soft color and silky finish reflect sunlight, creating a glowing ambience. For privacy, a pleated shade or roller blind can be mounted to the inside of the window.

OPPOSITE: The embroidered threads of this duvet evoke the exotic imagery of North African caravans laden with salt and gold. Although not inexpensive, silk is both luxurious and light as a feather—a perfect fabric for duvet covers. Place your quilt inside and it's like sleeping under a cloud. This duvet features silk-embroidered fabric and is backed with a queen-size sheet; gold tassel trim adds a finishing touch. ABOVE: Silky gold trim adorning the duvet cover accentuates the fabric's color and texture. Small details such as piping, braiding, tassels, or other decorative trim on bed linens, sofa cushions, pillows, or drapery can make important contributions to the overall richness and visual impact of a room's decor.

WINDOW TREATMENTS

Beautiful windows with colorful fabric—the soft sunlight pouring in—can become the focal point of any room. Window treatments complete the look of a room, uniting the color, pattern, and texture of furnishings, walls, floors, and accessories. Simplicity is essential to African-style window decoration. That doesn't, however, have to mean plain or

ABOVE: This decorative linen is a light and beautiful solution. Such natural fibers reflect the organic, earthbound feel of African style. They are especially beautiful in African country interiors. RIGHT: There are many ways in which we can experience the beauty of African art and design anew. Soft monochromatic Asoke textile in shades of cream and caramel is paired with heavy linen pillow shams, embroidered with the ram's horn Adinkra symbol. Simple eyelet-trimmed sheets and a waffle weave cotton bedspread add to the mix of color and pattern. The pillow shams are designed by Inside Design, Ltd.

cheap. Simplicity means that fabrics and fibers reflect the pared-down quality of African design, that drapes and curtains fold softly and have a fresh, natural quality.

Different treatments will conjure up different areas of the diverse continent. Bamboo, reed, wood, twig, raffia, or straw is perfect for blinds and screens, conjuring up images of equatorial Africa. For a casual look of East Africa, consider fabrics such as canvas, loosely woven linen, cotton, or cotton muslin. With any window treatment, remember to let the outside in—don't overpower the window with the treatment.

Light fabrics in a range of pastel colors will evoke North Africa—the soft desert winds, turbaned and veiled inhabitants, caravans of camels, and bustling outdoor markets of Tunisia, Morocco, and Algeria. Fabrics should be draped over curtain rods and swagged, knotted, or tied back to give rooms an element of romance and drama. Cotton, linen, silk, organza, damask, satin, and other translucent fabrics hold their shape without being stiff and flow luxuriously to the floor. Pastels in stripes, paisley, or intricate geometric patterns capture the exotic Afro-Islamic influences of the area. Tassels,

ABOVE: There is also a place for sheer fabrics when interpreting the look of Africa. Pattern and color can be reserved for upholstery, carpets, lamps, even floors and walls, leaving window treatments as a neutral element. Keep the treatment itself simple, dressing it up with tiebacks, decorative trims, or piping made of African prints or raffia. Here, the curtain rod and finial are garden gate accessories, purchased from an ironsmith.

trims, and tiebacks will enhance this North African elegance. Wrought iron, metal, and wood are good choices for curtain rods and rings; they will keep the look simple and add an organic touch to your windows.

You have a host of fabrics to choose from if you want to create a West African look: richly dyed indigo cloth, earthy Ewe cloth, and the classical Kente cloth are just a few. Window treatments should be celebratory. Use bright, vivid colors that reflect the rhythms of a village marketplace where women bustle about clad in bright colors from head to toe. Blends of linen and silk, cotton blends, even synthetic blends of polyester and acrylic work well, allowing you to take advantage of rich new textures and colors such as gold and copper. Don't skimp on panel width for this formal style of window treatment; use generous amounts of fabric. But think twice about using woven African textiles as panel fabric for window treatments—it can be very costly and could make too overpowering a statement. Instead, fashion cornices, valances, and tiebacks out of traditional African fabrics. It's a far less expensive alternative, and you will maintain the balance in the room between disparate design elements. Complete the West African look with tiebacks in wood, copper, or brass fashioned into the Adinkra symbols or other motifs characteristic of the regions.

Evoking Central Africa, a region known for its rain forests and strong tradition of ancestor worship, requires a more subtle approach to window treatment. The woven raffia produced by the Showa, the Kuba, the Pende, and the Akela people comes in a range of brown and beige tones. A monochromatic Central African color scheme requires subtle window treatments in shades such as black, beige, sage, mustard, or plum. The geometric designs of the region's textiles call for a modern, almost masculine approach to windows. Chenille, raw silk, mohair, cashmere, velvet, and linen are all appropriately rough in texture but still refined enough for this simple-tailored look.

Mixing Fabrics

Selecting a variety of fabrics to complement your African style will give your rooms a comfortable, natural ambience. The blend of diverse elements will ensure that your home won't feel like a museum. You don't have to fill a room with all things African to create an African look.

The key to mixing fabrics is to coordinate them in terms of color, pattern, and texture. For example, Asoke and Ewe textiles are soft and light and of fine quality. Their best match would be a fabric, such as fine wool, of the same high quality and delicate weave. Mud cloth, Showa fabric, and Kuba textiles have distinctive designs, neutral colors, and knobby textures. Coordinated fabrics—loose-weave linens, heavy cottons, even leather, velvets, suedes, or corduroys—should have a tailored, masculine feel that plays off the monochromatic tones and geometric patterns. The rough quality of raffia works well with heavier linens, chenille, raw silk, velvet, even mohair. The design project at hand best determines the coordinating colors and patterns. Depending on your color scheme, you might opt for contrasting hues and patterns or a more subtle tone-on-tone arrangement. If you opt for contrast, keep it under control. For example, mix silks, satins, and other luxury fabrics of contrasting colors with silky Kente.

When incorporating African textiles into your design scheme, think about both cost and aesthetics. Less can often be more. You don't have to make curtains or upholster your furniture with African fabric; instead, use it to cover valances and cornices, or make pillows and throws. Remember, too, that non-African fabrics mix well with African textiles and highlight their distinctive character. African textiles are available in such a wide range of patterns, textures, and colors. Pick the ones you like and start your African revival from seat to ceilings.

LEFT: The beauty of African textile design lies in the panorama of woven, printed, stamped, or batiked patterns and motifs. This Kente textile, now a bedspread, mingles with a parade of other patterns and colors, including mud cloth from Mali and cotton prints from the Ivory Coast. Combining authentic African textiles with versatile contemporary cottons can increase your decorating options in terms of both function and style.

before

Fabrics can add character to a room, revealing your style, down to the smallest of details. Here picture frames take on a life of their own when they are covered in fabric. They are no longer simply receptacles for photographs. They capture the eye in and of themselves.

after

African-Style
Padded Window Cornices

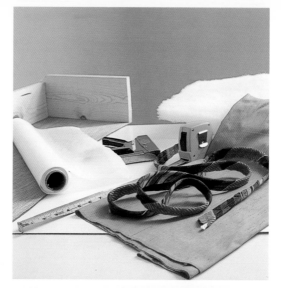

Padded window cornices can serve to unite the colors and patterns of disparate design elements such as upholstery, tablecloths, and pillows. And they are one of the most economical and elegant ways to work with African textiles. Since the amount of fabric used is minimal, you can even consider using the most expensive woven fabrics, such as strip weaves and mud cloths. Keep in mind, however, that the construction of the cornice frame itself should be left to an experienced carpenter.

Materials

Tape measure	Staple gun
Tracing paper	Fabric to cover cornice
Plywood	Piping trim (optional)
Quilt batting	

Creating the Cornices

1. Measure the width of your window from one end of the window frame to the other. In length, your cornice should be approximately one-quarter as long as the height of your window.

2. You can create a symmetrical pattern for your cornice by folding in half a piece of tracing paper that is half the width of your window. Trace out your design for the cornice on the tracing paper. Then lay the tracing paper on the plywood. Wooden cornices can be simply produced, but because they require power tools, rely on someone who can safely and professionally shape and assemble them.

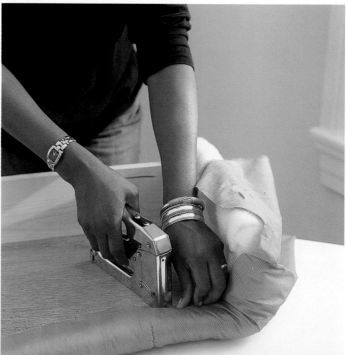

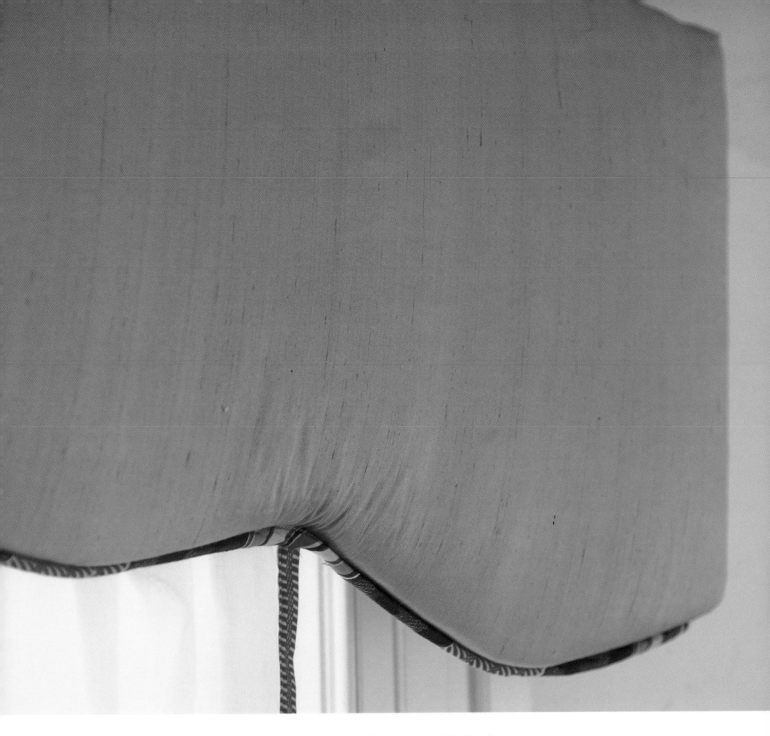

3. Attach 8-inch deep-side panels of plywood to the front panel.
4. Lay batting on top of the cornice and cut to size. Staple around the bottom, sides, and top, following the lines of the cornice. The staples should be one inch apart. Keep the batting smooth and tight as you staple.
5. Once the cornice is covered with the batting, you are ready to cut your main fabric. Trace the lines of the cornice on the fabric and, when cutting this fabric, allow 3 to 4 inches to fold over and attach to the back of your cornice.
6. Stretch the main fabric over the contours of the cornice and neatly staple the fabric to the back and sides of the cornice.
7. If you wish to add piping trim to the bottom of your cornice, attach free-hand with needle and thread.

Furniture

Until recently, most people in the United States could view African design only in art books, travel magazines, museums, and galleries. It was very rarely presented as a unique and distinctive interior design style with a consistent design profile. No wonder people found it next to impossible to make the conceptual leap from museum displays to home decorating, let alone to creating their own personal sense of African style. Today there is a wealth of furnishings, accessories, art, and images to inspire us. But furniture still seems to be the missing link for many people who want to create contemporary interpretations of African style.

Home owners and design professionals alike find that choosing just the right piece of furniture for any style of interior design can be a formidable challenge. There are technical concerns, such as selecting the appropriate lines, scale, proportions, and function. Then there are aesthetic decisions, such as choosing harmonious styles, fabrics, and finishes. The room itself is also an important factor. Is the space small or large? Does it have high or low ceilings? What kind of sunlight does the room get? Is wall space interrupted by large windows, doorways, built-in bookcases, or fireplaces? Such details will affect your furniture choices. The decisions are complex, but composing a furniture plan is another opportunity to flesh out your own interpretation of African style.

Africa has a long and rich history of furniture design, which first flourished in ancient Egypt. There, some of the

PRECEDING PAGES (LEFT): A twenty-year-old hand-carved chair from Tanzania is representative of the organic beauty of East African furniture. The concave carved seat and the central base support that splays out to form three legs are the hallmarks of stools and chairs from this region. Note the subtle, uneven carved surface, the easy curve of the seat and back, and the minimal geometric pattern.
BELOW: The easy curves and tapered chunky legs of this hand-carved lounge bench produced by the Tiv artisans of Nigeria create a progressive simplicity that makes the piece timeless. It is as much at home with modern furniture as it is in a traditional African setting.

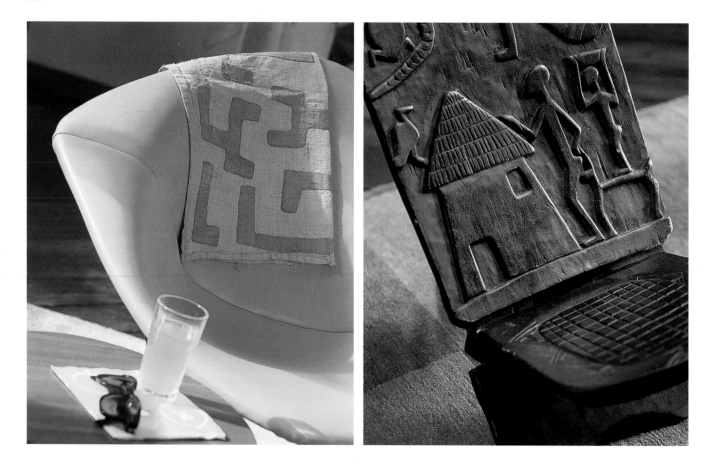

most innovative furniture ever produced was designed and manufactured as early as 3100 B.C. for royalty. Examples include tables inlaid with mother-of-pearl, beds made of ebony with footboards covered in heavy gold sheeting, ivory stools with woven leather seats, and even beds that could be folded up for travel. But furnishing your home in African style does not mean that you must use all things African. When interpreting African style for contemporary homes, we need to satisfy the functional demands of modern life. We need soft furnishings, such as sofas, upholstered chairs, and sleep sofas, and we must have dining tables, entertainment centers, and cabinetry of all kinds. To meet these requirements, look beyond Africa to your favorite furniture styles. Introducing furnishings from different times and places into your home is a great way to create an original and exciting interior—and still evoke the spirit of Africa.

ABOVE LEFT: A leather and wire chair created by furniture designer and sculptor Harry Bertoia in 1950 is a study in organic form. Its innovative design harmonizes with African forms. ABOVE RIGHT: Functional design and the ancient tradition of carving come together in this two-piece hand-sculpted lounge chair produced by the Dogon people in Mali. Like most African furniture, it sits low to the ground. Its simple and clever assembly has made it a favorite of designers and collectors. OPPOSITE: This unusual handwoven basket/hamper from Senegal and Russell Woodard's wire chair, designed in the 1950s, share soft colors and soft lines. Chair from America Antiques & Design.

How Africa Makes Foreign Furniture Its Own

While traveling throughout West Africa, I noticed that many people had combinations of traditional and contemporary furnishings in their homes. Against a background of sofas, upholstered armchairs, and cabinetry of European or Arabic influence, they set African stools in a wide range of styles, chairs of different types, and other accent furnishings made of wood, leather, bamboo, or cane.

Over the centuries, colonial occupation brought a host of cultural influences to the continent of Africa. The Dutch, British, Italians, Germans, Lebanese, Indians, Arabs, and others found their way to Africa's shores and left their mark. Africans were exposed to new and different ways of doing things and looking at the world. But the continent's culture, so deeply grounded in its history and religions, always resisted domination and assimilation, tempering the effects of occupation and colonialism with its own artistic traditions. Therefore, whenever the African people adopted foreign ideas, they put their own spin on them. Nowhere is this approach more evident than in their interpretation of furniture. An attention to function and simplicity and a reverence for nature distinguish furniture as Africa's own.

There are few design requirements for furniture befitting African style. Color, finish, and form can vary according to

RIGHT: The curvaceous and sculptural furniture from the 1940s and 1950s echoes the organic free-form of African masks and furnishings. A mud cloth textile from Mali was chosen to cover the cushions of this vintage IKEA leather sofa. Three stackable tables with simple sculptured legs serve the purpose of a coffee table. The two accompanying chairs are works of art in and of themselves: one is a traditional two-piece Dogon lounge chair from Mali, and the other is an original Diamond chair by Harry Bertoia. The Dogon chair is from Pearl of Africa and the Bertoia chair is from Mode Moderne. Handwoven carpet designed by Barbara Barry available at Tufenkian Tibetan Carpets.

ABOVE: Recycle to create your own interpretation of African style. One of my mother's favorites, this 1930s easy chair was the perfect candidate for an African revival. Over the years, it had fallen on hard times: although structurally sound, it had become the cat's favorite scratching post. But with a bit of imagination, access to the right upholstery fabrics, and a skillful upholsterer, her gorgeous old piece became a star again. This contemporary African textile is designed by Dan Sekanwagi for Visual Feast Fabrics.

your own taste. But always keep in mind that comfort is as important as aesthetics. A chair, stool, sofa, table, or bed headboard should be as relaxing to use as it is beautiful to view. Also, the function of every piece should be obvious, even if the piece is multi-functional. There is a style of furniture for every personality. A few general approaches to selecting the right furniture can help you narrow down the options.

Do-It-Yourself Furniture

The first approach is to do it yourself and use what you already have. Don't discard wonderful, well-made furniture just because it is old. That favorite chair you inherited from your grandmother and the bed frame you found at a flea market are ripe for rein-carnation into a second, African life. Recycling existing furniture through the use of fabric, pattern, paint, and adornment is the perfect way to preserve cherished pieces in a fresh new way. You can use Africa's abundance of textiles, patterns, symbols, and decorative objects to transform your furniture into African style.

FABRIC

Authentic African textiles produced on the continent and African-inspired fabrics pro-duced here in the United States offer many options for hands-on recycling. You can choose from an ever-growing assortment of prints and patterns for upholstery and slip-covers. African textiles in an array of color combinations, patterns, and textures will gloriously transform your otherwise ordinary furniture. As a casual throw over a sofa, as accent pillows, or placed on a table, African textiles instantaneously give new life to furniture.

PATTERN AND PAINT

Painted patterns have the power to create drama and richness when applied to furni-ture. African patterns, such as a Kuba configuration or a Yoruba animal motif, can radi-cally reinvigorate a piece and give it new focus. Before painting tables, cabinets, or any other wood-frame furnishings, consider the scale and proportion of the furniture as well as the pattern's intensity of color and scale. Color or a combination of colors will determine whether a single pattern or a collection of patterns becomes the focus:

decide on a single motif or a collection of motifs, patterns that are organic or geometric, intricate or free-form; then express your designs in soft, muted hues for a mellow effect, or use strong, contrasting hues for a more dramatic look.

ADORNMENT

To adorn means to add beauty, to enhance, or to make pleasing, attractive, or impressive. If ever there was a place where life is richly celebrated through design, where adornment has evolved into an elaborate art form permeating every aspect of life and culture, it is Mother Africa. Let your imagination run free and create a look rich in artistic tradition through the use of adornment. Trims, feathers, tassels, ribbons, beads, shells, raffia, and rope are just a few materials that can express the spirit of Africa. Improvisational finishing touches—piping on chair cushions, decorative trinkets on standing screens, handles, and pulls for cabinetry—add glamour, sophistication, wit, and personality to a piece of furniture aching for new life. They are like the great pair of earrings that completes an outfit.

LEFT: Each of these pillows says Africa in its own way. Luxurious silk adds sophistication and glamour; smooth, soft feathers lend an exotic touch. Don't be afraid to experiment and adorn your furnishings with feathers, buttons, beads, shell, or raffia. These are from Inside Design, Ltd.

LEFT: Colorful beads or buttons can redefine your furnishings. These small beads are connected with fine wire and attached to a lamp shade frame. Add decorative trim or ribbon to conceal wire if necessary. BELOW RIGHT: Beads tell the history of the continent's trade and its cultural relationship with Europe and the Middle East. Highly valued throughout ancient African cultures, beads made of clay, shell, stone, and metal were produced there as early as 10,000 B.C. Beginning in the fifteenth century, glass beads and bottles were imported from Europe and the Middle East. The bottles were crushed and recycled to make new beads in diverse styles to satisfy the African market. BELOW LEFT: This young Turkana woman wears a traditional high-collar necklace of bold, contrasting colors. Such creations are easily a wonderful source of inspiration.

Furniture That Makes the African Connection

A second approach to selecting furniture for African style is to look for pieces that, although not African-inspired in and of themselves, nevertheless have a particular quality or design element that is characteristic of African design. Choose furniture that has a handmade or organic quality—maybe a table made of mahogany, rosewood, or bamboo; chairs and sofas with seats made of sea grass, rope, wicker, cane, or leather; and bed frames of copper, brass, or wrought iron. Here the African-inspired elements are the natural materials and fibers: all are used in traditional African art. Such materials convey a relaxed look and have a rich tactile quality. For example, inexpensive wicker armchairs with cushions covered in African prints echo the earthy charm of Africa in such a simple, understated way.

You can also opt for furniture with sculptural forms and curved lines, mirroring the African tradition of hand-carved design. Architectural details, masks, figurines, chairs, stools, and other objects possess this organic and sculptured characteristic. Think of the soft curved lines as a seductive and sensual invitation to comfort. Seat backs that are molded into arms, seats and backs sculpted as a single whole, leg supports that spring from the same source and fan out, seats with a subtle scoop in the middle and upward curve

LEFT: In the spirit of Afro Retro, this mahogany dining room ensemble combines African textile and sculptural forms from Zaire's Kasai River valley with 1940s American pieces. The furniture form is simple and light, with tapered and splayed legs—a hallmark of mid-century modern design. Showa mats woven of dyed raffia give the chair seats a new African life. An exquisitely carved throwing knife from Zaire and the graphic placement of three masks add to the minimalist interpretation of Afro Retro. The furniture is from America Antiques and Design. The painting is by Albert Kness.

on the sides—these are just some of the furniture forms you can consider to complement African furnishing and accessories.

African-Inspired Furniture

A final approach, and very often the most expensive one, is to look for furniture explicitly inspired by Africa. Classic pieces from the European Empire period of the late nineteenth century reflect the influences of early Egyptian furnishings. Art Deco furniture of the 1920s interpreted Africa through a veil of glamour and luxury, using materials such as ivory, tortoiseshell, snakeskin, zebra pelts, and leopard skins. Modern organic furnishings of the 1940s and 1950s

ABOVE: This traditional wingback chair is covered with a fabric that I found unexpectedly while browsing in a local fabric store. Luckily, there was enough for two chairs.
RIGHT: Chunky, curvaceous, and worn with use, a Senufo wash stool meets its match in a contemporary African-inspired handwoven carpet. Although the two pieces come from different parts of the world, they still speak to each other. Carpet available at Tufenkian Tibetan Carpets.

responded to the lure of Africa by way of Cubism, their forms and lines mirroring the abstract simplicity of African design.

Consider the Art Deco period. Inspired in part by African art forms such as the ceremonial mask, many designers of the time mimicked the design of the continent in the exotic elegance of their furnishings—simple curves and rich, dark, tropical woods such as ebony, mahogany, teak, and rosewood; mother-of-pearl inlays; and decorative veneers. Hallmarks of this style are geometric motifs and symbols. The most popular is the Egyptian sunrise motif, which can be found on everything from radios to bed frames to architecture. Anne Massey writes in *Interior Design of the 20th Century,* "This symbol was probably derived from Egyptian art, a popular source of inspiration after the discovery of Tutankhamen's tomb in 1922."

One of Cubism's most important sources of inspiration was non-European art, and Art Deco designers used the same sources to create an exotic style. Designers such as Pierre Legrain, Paul Theodore Frankl, Eileen Gray, and Jean-Michel Frank were influenced by African furnishings at different points in their careers, sometimes creating exact reproductions of traditional African chairs and stools. For example, Legrain's Tabouret Ashanti chair imitates the design of chairs produced by the Tiv artisans of Nigeria. Some of the furniture from this period is oversize and chunky, but much of it possesses the simple lines that chime perfectly with African art.

The inherently modern quality of African art and design fits beautifully with the furniture designs from the 1940s and 1950s. Charles and Ray Eames, Harry Bertoia, George Nelson, Eero Saarinen, and Finn Juhl mastered European technology of the day. They bent and molded wood and metal to produce chairs and sofas that resemble abstract sculpture. Harry Bertoia's diamond chair, Arne Jacobson's egg chair, and Isamu Noguchi's glass-and-walnut coffee table are some favorite examples of the biomorphic, free-form design characteristic of this period. For Finn Juhl, African art was a direct inspiration. The most sculptural of the Danish designers, he looked to tribal art and abstract organic sculpture as sources. Technology and art come together in his famous chieftain chair made of rosewood and leather.

OPPOSITE: At top, a small tortoise-shell bowl holding a single lily in full bloom complements the look of a contemporary wire drum table. Bottom: This multifunctional bench/coffeetable (without cushion) designed by Finn Juhl is one of his early pieces.

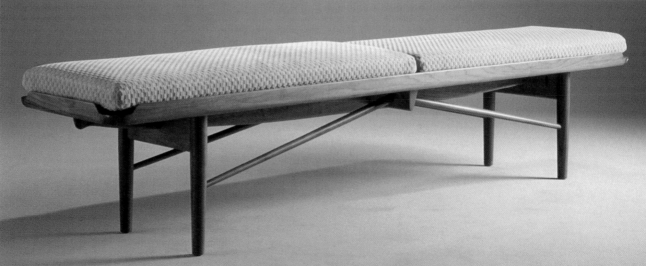

TOP AND BOTTOM RIGHT: Danish designer and decorator Finn Juhl, one of the foremost interpreters of Danish Modern furniture of the 1940s and 1950s, proudly acknowledged his debt to African art and design. In 1951, Juhl introduced Danish Modern to the United States with a line for Baker Furniture. His teak and leather Chieftain chair, shown here, reveals the influence of African style. This original chair is from Jacksons 20th-Century Design, Stockholm. Baker Furniture continues to produce it, as well as other pieces by Juhl. TOP RIGHT: A rare collection of Finn Juhl originals: a set of six Egyptian chairs and a silver inlay dining table dubbed "Thirty Pieces of Silver." OPPOSITE: Ghanaian furniture designer Kwabena Smith clearly embraces the spirit of Sankofa in his Sahara table and chair. Smith incorporated a creative mix of materials, including Ghanaian Odum wood, hand-worked metal, mud cloth, and raffia, all of which celebrate contemporary West African style. The low seat and comfortable width offer a fresh take on design. Produced in Ghana, Smith's furniture line totals fifty-five original pieces. The furniture is available at Ashanti Origins. The lamp is from Lee's Studio.

Contemporary African Design

The beauty of African art lies in part with its timeless quality. The fact that it was considered modern and avant-garde to the visionary artists of the early 1900s and continues to be the choice of fine contemporary artists and designers in the early years of the twenty-first century is a testament to this. We look to classic African art for its design genius and exquisite craftsmanship. Fortunately, African art shares in the dynamic evolution of all art, always growing and creating new classics. Without abandoning traditional techniques, new African designers continue to build on the rich artistic legacy of the motherland, while at the same time reflecting the way we live today.

These new designers create for African markets as well as for international markets. Their work allows us to surround ourselves with beautiful and practical design solutions in the form of comfortable seating, handsome metalwork, practical storage, attractive tableware and lighting, and other home accessories. After centuries of anonymous master artists, finally we are able to give credit and recognition to talented African artists and craftsmen who create the new treasures of the twenty-first century. Designers such as Nigerian textile designer Adeshola Olaniyi, Cameroonian architect and furniture designer Epee Ellong for Padouk, Ghanaian furniture designer Kwabena Smith for Ashanti Origins, and Ugandan textile designer Dan Sekanwagi of Visual Feast Fabrics are just a few of the many contemporary African designers who are a part of the continuum of African art and design.

CHAIRS

Furniture designers focus on chairs more than any other form of furniture. They are the aesthetic and functional backbone of any interior. Entire books are dedicated to the chair, its significance in our lives and its evolution over the centuries. So much more than a place to sit, chairs enfold us in comfort and security. Rocking chairs soothe the stresses of the day, sumptuous leather easy chairs entice us to snuggle up with our favorite novel. You can place chairs anywhere around a room, and there is an abundance of chair designs to meet every decorating and functional need.

Chairs do not have the same rich history in Africa as stools do. The Egyptians produced exquisite pieces with X-frame supports and carved animal feet, but traditionally sub-Saharan Africans used stools in place of chairs, which were indigenous to other cultures. Nevertheless, chairs can be a perfect vehicle for conveying a contemporary sense of African design. Paint their frames, upholster them, add patterned pillows with designs, and use textiles as throws, and the chairs come to life.

When choosing the right chair for your interior, think first of function. It doesn't matter how good the chair looks if it doesn't fit the purpose of the space. What a waste of a comfy easy chair if you place it in a transitional space such as a foyer or a corridor. Similarly, stylized chairs that stress design rather than comfort are beautiful additions

LEFT: A contemporary Tunisian arm-chair, with a wrought-iron frame wrapped in bamboo and a sea grass-rope seat and back, has a compelling but understated design. Its North African origins make it a complementary addition to African-inspired interior settings. Available at Anthropologie. BELOW: A combination of Scandinavian light wood and traditional Ghanaian textile design creates a harmonious whole. The cloth features a pattern of a stool symbolizing hospitality and courtesy. Available at Kente Ventures, Inc.

chairs

TOP LEFT: Cameroonian architect and furniture designer Epee Ellong continues the tradition of hand-carved symbolic and decorative design. His Mbango stool is made of Bete tropical wood from Central Africa. BOTTOM LEFT: The Mbango stool, or Elephant stool, is elaborately carved but surprisingly lightweight. Dyed woven raffia covers a swayed seat with a low decorative back support. These are available at Padouk Design.

stools

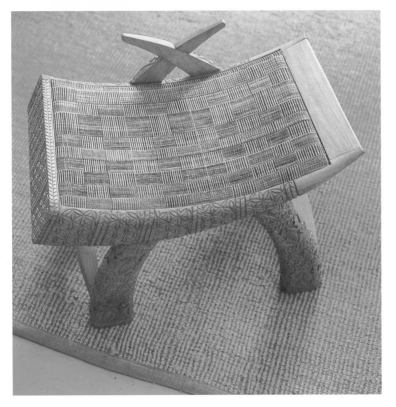

ABOVE: Ellong fashions contemporary furniture in traditional African style, using natural materials. His cube-shaped ottoman is upholstered in hand-woven raffia. Its height makes it appropriate as dining seating or as accent furniture in living rooms. Available at Padouk Design. OPPOSITE: A close-up of the ottoman's design: the raffia upholstery cover is finished off with a fringe skirt; the leg support is wrapped in sea grass.

to any living room, but make sure you have plenty of comfortable seating as well. When selecting your chairs, keep in mind that lower, wider pieces with softer lines, so characteristic of traditional African furnishings, will help create that connection to Africa.

TABLES

While seldom the focal point of a room, tables are a natural point of gravitation, inviting us to gather and relax. From coffee and end tables to accent and dining tables, they are essential to the social life of a home. Coffee tables are practical and serve a social function like no other piece of furniture, whether gathering for cocktails with friends before an evening out or relaxing with the Sunday newspaper at the end of a long week. There is no standard size for a coffee table; as long as they meet the functional and aesthetic demands of the room, the sky is the limit. Choose from wood, rattan, metal, leather, or glass; square, round, rectangular, or triangular. Traditional African pieces, such as a carved wooden Tiv bench, a Senufo bed, or woven Egyptian tables, are great options; works of art and practical furniture, these sculptural low-slung designs are beautiful for displaying accessories. More familiar, taller coffee tables are more convenient for family rooms, libraries, or for serving food and drinks. A versatile approach can be created by grouping several smaller tables or stacking tables.

STOOLS

Stools are among the most significant of African art forms. Carved in a variety of designs, motifs, and symbols—from intricately elaborate Cameroonian stools to minimalist Senufo stools—they communicate social status, ethnic and religious affiliation, and ancestral ties. No matter their size, style, or purpose, all African stools are fashioned from a single piece of wood and exude the spiritual force of trees. These pieces are so simple and basic that they can be considered sculptures.

Traditional African stools sit low to the ground, with a wide base and a concave seat. They are portable, comfortable, and inviting—the perfect option for casual living room seating at a party or any other social gathering. They can also function as side tables and footstools. And because they are usually no more than 15 inches high, they can easily be stored under a coffee table when not in use. To decide how to use stools in your interior, take your cue from Africa. There, stools are used wherever people gather—

TOP LEFT: Color, geometry, texture, and form intermingle in the "Modern West African Table," produced by decorative painter Cheryl Levin and metalsmith Bob Phillips. The table is decorated with a colorful pattern that is hand-painted with casein paints. The sculptured frame is made of wrought iron. Available at Phillips Metal. ABOVE: The graceful "Corinthian" table by Levin and Phillips also evokes images of North Africa. This is available at Phillips Metal. LEFT: Juhl's table/bench, made of sycamore, is included in Baker's Finn Juhl collection. BOTTOM RIGHT: This Arobaini table, from the island of Lamu, is hand-carved of solid mahogany. The geometric Bjuni patterns and generous leg supports reveal a mixture of African, Arab, and European influences. This is available at Lamu Industries. BOTTOM LEFT: A console table and small coffee table are also made on the island of Lamu. This is available at Lamu Industries.

tables

around a fire, in a kitchen, and even outdoors milking cattle or washing clothes on the bank of a river. As footstools, side tables, or extra seating, they are just as versatile and portable in the bedroom, living room, and family room of a contemporary home.

SOFAS

Like no other furnishing, sofas communicate their owners' personalities. People take nearly as much care in purchasing a sofa as they do in buying a car. And sofas can be a major expense, so many will make countless visits to showrooms before finally deciding on the perfect piece. If you are shopping for a sofa, pay close attention to size. Do three people really enjoy sitting on that one long sofa? Ask the person in the middle. Maybe you would prefer two love seats. If you like to curl up and read in the corner, make sure the armrests are high. Maybe you prefer to stretch out and nap; if so, you need low armrests and several accompanying pillows. Color and pattern are also critical considerations when choosing large pieces of furniture such as sofas. Consult your color board and furniture plan, and make sure that your sofa harmonizes with the overall vision of your interior.

Choosing a sofa of any design style is difficult, but finding a sofa inspired by Africa is a real rarity. When was the last time you saw one upholstered in African textiles or African-inspired fabrics? Sofas, because of their sheer size, often become the focal point of a room, and many fear that such a large piece of furniture covered with patterns and colors will simply be too overpowering. If you are one to shy away from bold design statements, try one solid color or a combination of monochromatic neutrals, such as cream, beige, and sepia; or soft pastels, such as tropical pink, blue, and green. These hues will quietly evoke an African ambience. Add traditional African throws or pillows covered in African-inspired patterns to complete the look.

Selecting furniture can be a real challenge, even for a professional. So stay focused on your functional needs, consult your color board and furniture plan, and look for guidance to the source of your inspiration: African stools, ceremonial masks, textiles, architecture, and accessories. Be resourceful. Don't hunt for sofas only in showrooms. Search through auctions, antique stores, and even flea markets for those priceless furniture finds.

before

A bit of paint and fabric can make a big difference. Take this simple, unpainted folding chair—always useful when you need additional dining chairs for casual family-style dinners. First, I painted the chair, applying a base coat and following it with a second after it had dried. Next, using 1½ yards of an African print fabric imported from the Ivory Coast, I made a simple sleeve to fit over the chair back. Then I covered a cushion that was designed to fit the seat. Decorate one or two of these chairs for a small kitchen space, or twenty of them in an array of colors and fabrics for a festive party.

after

Using Showa Mats for
Seat Cushions

You don't need to send those dining room chairs off to be professionally reupholstered in order to inject them with African style. Instead, try doing it yourself! As long as the seat cushion is easily removed from the body of the chair, you can achieve a professional African look at home.

Materials

Full-size Showa raffia woven mats (usually 21 to 24 inches square)

Seat cushions

Staple gun

Covering the Cushion

1. Disassemble chair and remove seat cushion.
2. Place Showa mat facedown, and lay seat cushion facedown on top of it.
3. Fold sides of fabric up and staple the fabric to the back of the seat. Check to see that the pattern is positioned evenly across the seat cushion as you staple.
4. Reassemble chair.

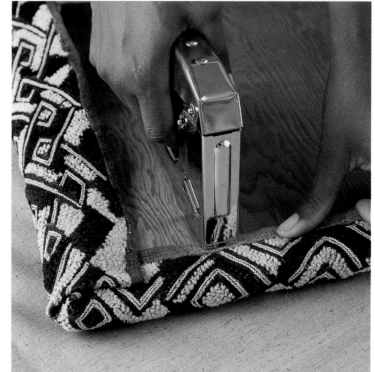

Headboard
Covered in African Textile

With this padded headboard, you can fall asleep enveloped in Africa. You'll have to hire a carpenter to help you with the first stage of the project: making the headboard. Make sure you specify the shape you want—square or rounded corners, simple or more elaborate shapes. Plywood is perfect for a project like this, as it comes in large standard sheets of 4 x 8 feet. Have your carpenter finish off the edges of the headboard with 2- x 3-inch pieces of wood to give it a more substantial look and feel.

Materials

Quilt batting	Upholstery fabric
Headboard	Staple gun

Creating the Headboard

1. Lay the quilt batting on the floor. Make sure it is smooth and flat. Place headboard on top of the batting, facedown.
2. Bring batting up around the edges of the headboard and cut to shape. Leave at least 1½ inches of extra batting, and staple it securely to the 2 x 3s.
3. Repeat steps 1 and 2 with the upholstery fabric.
4. Have your carpenter mount the headboard directly and securely to the wall.

Accessories *and* Display

We tell a thousand stories about
ourselves and our experiences through
the things that surround us. African
style celebrates those life experiences
and unites them with a love of all
things African. Combining the old
and new, the rough and refined,
family history and African culture, is
a recipe for beautiful design. Family
photos, documents, and letters;

soft patchwork quilts made from a mix of African textiles and childhood clothing; stools, sculpture, pottery, collectibles, and mementos—objects and accessories transport the past into the present and make a room our own.

Too many people think about accessories only after all the big-ticket items have been purchased and arranged in freshly painted rooms. But accessories and display are integral to any design scheme and should be part of your overall vision for your space from the outset. In the planning stages of the decorating process, take an inventory of all those bowls, baskets, pieces of fabric, and other treasures. Let your sense of fantasy, romance, and drama take flight with the things that mean the most to you.

You have many options for accessorizing in African style: you can purchase traditional African art, contemporary reproductions, or African-inspired home accessories produced in Europe and the United States—or you can roll up your sleeves and make your own.

Whereas traditional African art is more popular than ever, African-inspired china, upholstery fabrics, carpets, and other home accessories are not

PRECEDING PAGES: The subtle yet exciting color scheme and free-form geometric pattern of this African-inspired five-piece table setting captures the contemporary feeling of Africa. Designed by Laurie Gates, it is available at Blackberry. The tray is available at Merit Ventures. We should only collect the things we love. A Philadelphia townhouse preserves the memory of a family's past. To the right is a framed piece of a handmade quilt made by a great grandmother. A childhood photo, souvenirs, and flowers create an intimate collection of personal treasures.

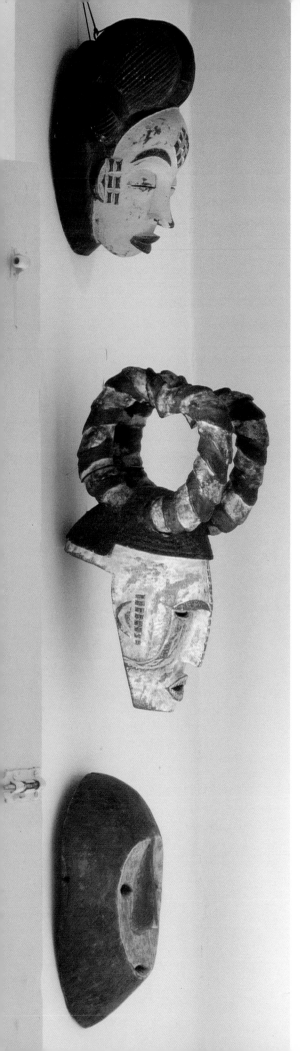

always readily available, and they can be quite expensive when they are. In the tradition of African artists and craftsmen, it's best to be resourceful and take a hands-on approach to accessories.

African Art and Crafts

Africa is home to an abundance of traditional arts, crafts, and accessories that can help you evoke the spirit of the continent. Throughout Africa, people have created decorative arts and crafts that speak to every aspect of life—religious worship, rites of passage, history, architecture, entertainment, decoration, and personal adornment, to name a few. Each country has its own unique style of design reflected through its decorative and functional arts.

The history of the decorative arts in Africa dates back at least to 2200 B.C. The Egyptians designed fine furnishings and accessories more than 5,000 years ago using techniques that are still practiced today the world over, such as wood inlaying, gold leafing, decorative faux painting, embroidery, and appliqué. The ancient Nubians, who lived to the south of Egypt, have recently been documented and recognized for their contributions to the decorative and utilitarian arts. The Nok of Nigeria sculpted

LEFT: Masks are the quintessence of African art; they are a "must have" for African-inspired interiors. Whether the focus is on a single mask, which makes an impressive statement, or on a collection, masks are the spirit of Africa. Before finalizing a wall display for your masks, experiment with a variety of layouts by placing them on the floor until you are satisfied. Collections, whether small or large, create a stronger visual impact when arranged in some formation, as opposed to placing them randomly throughout the room. The masks are available at Pearl of Africa.

ABOVE LEFT: From South Africa to Tunisia, African basket designs are endlessly appealing. Used for food storage, and as hampers and trays, they can be as practical in our homes as they are in Africa. This double-handled basket is from East Africa. LEFT: A decorative brass cup produced in West Africa is designed by Frederic Alcantara for Bamboula, Ltd. It captures the rough and refined essence of African design. Perfect on a dining table, the cup can hold fruits, snacks, or a small bouquet of flowers. Or why not turn it into a desk accessory and fill it with pencils and pens? ABOVE: Though powerful-looking, a Baule mask from the Ivory Coast creates a serene air in the bedroom in which it hangs.

ABOVE: An adobe Dogon mask finds a home on a hand-carved Nigerian stool produced by the Nupe. Whether formally displayed or casually placed, African art objects can be the focus of any interior. The stool and mask are available at Indigo Arts. OPPOSITE: Clay pots can be displayed as a collection or used as planters or containers in any area of the home. Clockwise from top: A four-sided Ghanaian plant pot embossed with the ram's horn Adinkra symbol; a contemporary pot made by a female potter from the Ivory Coast (it is said that the face came to her in a dream); a decorative clay pot from Ghana with rope-stitched ornamentation; and a large three-footed cooking pot of varying tones and simple decorative detailing from the Lake Victoria region of Kenya. Rope-stitch pot from Bamboula, Ltd., other pots from Garden Traditions.

naturalistic heads out of stone and terra-cotta as early as 500 B.C. And the Akan of the Ivory Coast and Ghana created an art form out of the most functional of objects— small weights for measuring gold dust. According to "Elmina Art and Trade on the West African Coast," "Akan artists delighted in creating miniature depictions of the world around them. Not only are the weights splendid works in themselves, they also comment on the history and thought of the people who used them." It is this love of the small things that says so much about a people, and such attention to style down to the details is the true legacy of African style.

Today African art is experiencing a revival. There is so much out there to buy that you really have to do your research before you commit to a purchase. Search your local bookstore for the many excellent publications on the history and background of African masks, sculptures, textiles, and other art forms. These books will give you a strong introduction to the world of African art. The next decision should be whether to purchase older or more contemporary works—the difference in price can be in the thousands of dollars. As demand for older African art mounts, much is being written about determining its authenticity. If you feel unprepared to make such appraisals on your own, seek the services of reputable art dealers who will guarantee the authenticity of any work they sell. It can be hard to distinguish what is old from what looks old, so my advice is to consult with the professionals. And remember that masks, sculptures, and textiles that are fifty years old and more are becoming increasingly rare, so prices are soaring accordingly.

Art produced by today's craftsmen can be a more affordable alternative. In fact, age and authenticity are not always the most important criteria when selecting masks, fig-urines, and sculptures for interior design. Consider instead design form, aesthetic character, size, color, and general condition. Some of my favorite masks are Dan masks from the Ivory Coast and Fang masks of the Dogon. Both have very elegant designs, simple subtle lines, and smooth polished finishes in woods ranging from black ebony to white ash. These masks are quite simply beautiful—it doesn't matter whether they are five or fifty years old, their basic design never changes.

ABOVE: Increasingly, artifacts from African countries are produced for markets abroad. These decorative trays combine traditional and modern manufacturing techniques. Without spending a lot of money, you have easily set the stage for a great table by using these trays. Simply cover the table with a cotton print and add colorful plates and a bouquet of fresh flowers. RIGHT: In the Ogowe River region in Gabon, artisans and sculptors produce their own signature white-faced mask designs, which symbolize the afterworld and are used for funeral ceremonies. Masks are from Pearl of Africa.

Everyday Accessories

ABOVE LEFT: Traditional West African
symbols were the inspiration for this
beautiful brass hardware, which can be
used for everyday function as handles
for drawers, doors, or boxes. The hardware is from Bamboula, Ltd. ABOVE
RIGHT: Practical accessories, such as
switch plates, can also be decorative
accents that coordinate with other
elements in the room and capture the
essence of Africa. Accessories are from
Harris, The Rarest SwitchPlate.
OPPOSITE: More than ever before,
African-inspired products are readily
available. Choose from objects such as
a decorative calabash or a hand-
decorated cowrie shell container basket
produced by the Hausa of Nigeria from
Craft Caravan, or a brass-studded bowl
and cup by Frederic Alcantara for
Bamboula, Ltd.

Africa produces a wide variety of home accessories in colors
and designs that mix freely with contemporary color palettes
and lifestyles. Trays from Morocco made of copper, silver, or
wood; bowls and vases from Senegal covered in brass; contemporary mud cloths from Mali woven into bedspreads;
cushioned stools of woven raffia from Cameroon; pots from
East Africa, their legs etched with ancestral markings—the
options are endless. A collection of brass, copper, or
wrought-iron candleholders adorned with beads and stones is
a great table display. An arrangement of ceramics, pottery,
gourds, trays, and platters filled with fruits, fresh greens, and
tropical flowers creates an island of natural beauty.

Many African-inspired items, from tableware to occasional
furniture, are manufactured closer to home. Artists and

designers—from Picasso, Matisse, and Modigliani to Pierre Legrain, Emile-Jacques Ruhlmann, and Finn Juhl—were influenced by the primeval forms of African art and design. Today African-inspired accessories—tableware, bed linens, accent furniture, and more—can be found at boutiques, specialty stores, and selected retail stores and galleries. Still, you might find your choices to be somewhat limited unless you are willing to try your hand at making some accessories yourself.

DO-IT-YOURSELF DESIGN

If you want a duvet cover made of African fabric, why not make it yourself? Curtains and other window treatments such as valances and cornices may need some embellishing with piping, trims, or beadwork. Don't let the fact that no one has heard of an

ABOVE LEFT: Hermes's "Africa" china pattern creates a formal look. The Pyramid box in the background is from Merit Ventures. ABOVE RIGHT: An eclectic combination of baskets, beads, cowrie shells, straw mats, colorful plates, and fresh flowers creates a cheerful table setting. Every element does not have to be African, but keep your patterns and color schemes consistent. The place mats are from B.I.T.H. The plates are from Home Zone. OPPOSITE LEFT: Fresh flowers and fruit, twig mats and raffia, baskets and a decorated wood platter, and even a small stool work together to create an exotic, tropical feeling. The square pastel plates are from Home Zone; the twig mats are from Blackberry; and the basket, candleholders, and platter are from Bamboula, Ltd. OPPOSITE RIGHT: Tables are a great place to display vintage and new accessories. Beautiful, easy-to-care-for African-inspired place mats and napkins build a beautifully layered look, but they also add protection for the Asoke textile that covers this table. For a bit of sparkle, add brass containers, napkin rings, and gold chargers. The Asoke textile is from Beads of Paradise; the place mats and napkins are from B.I.T.H.; and the brass accessories are from Bamboula, Ltd.

African bed deter you. Make your own headboard from plywood, 2 x 4s, quilt batting, and your favorite African cloth. Making decorative frames for pictures and mirrors is a simple project that can be completed in a day.

You can make your own tablecloths, place mats, and napkins to express the spirit of Africa. Keep the fabric patterns simple. Choose a solid color for the tablecloth, and then look to the plethora of African prints in a variety of designs and patterns for your place mats, napkins, and runners. Just make sure the fabric is sturdy enough for repeated washing, and prewash it in cold water to see if the colors hold. Back place mats and runners with heavy washable fabric to give them a solid feel.

ACCENT FURNITURE

Traditional African stools, chairs, benches, doors, and beds are functional in design and an aesthetic delight. African stools are extremely versatile. They can be moved from room to room and used as footstools, side tables, or extra seating for guests. They come in different shapes and sizes, from Kenyan three-legged milking stools, only 8 inches high, to eight-legged Nupe stools from Nigeria; from the traditional Ghanaian Wisdom Knot stools to the classic Senufo wash stools. African chairs also have a unique design: splayed legs, scooped-out seats, and simple carved backs. Ethiopian and Kenyan chairs are utilitarian pieces of soulful sculpture.

FRESH FLOWERS

Fresh flowers are a critical accessory in any home, and they are an integral part of African style. Flowers add color, form, and fragrance to interiors. Arrangements created by florists are studied works of art, but even a trained florist appreciates the simplicity of a bouquet bundled in tissue paper or a single stem in just the right vase. A vase filled with small blooms will bring a breath of fresh air to a cluttered work desk. Indeed, flowers are meant for every room in the home. They make a joyful addition to tablescapes of books, framed photographs, or ceramic pieces.

Flowers that flourish wild in the tropical climates of Africa, such as bird of paradise and proteas, are too exotic to grow in certain climates but are seasonally available in flower shops the world over. Other plants such as black-eyed Susans, impatiens, daisies, and carpet geraniums are more familiar African derivatives. Delphiniums, ranunculuses, poppies, and lilacs, although not native to Africa, are perennial favorites and add rich purples and warm oranges to the mix. The elegant orchids, indigenous to South Africa, range in color from white to ruby red. Agapanthus forms a ball of lilac-colored blossoms at the end of a long slender stem. Rustic African pottery can offer a wonderful textural contrast to a graceful long-stemmed calla lily, and an East African pedestal bowl can be given new life when filled with a small round bouquet.

OPPOSITE: **Every accessory plays its part in the success of this dining setting. The cotton-woven Ewe cloth, with its lime greens, berry reds, banana yellow, pale pinks, and burnt oranges, is dazzling, and so are the dining chairs upholstered in Kente cloth. The chandelier is elegantly rustic, with a handmade quality, and the soft color of the lilacs creates an overall impression of sheer delight. The chandelier is from The Menagerie, Ltd. The chairs are from Kente Ventures, Inc.; the table linens are from B.I.T.H.; the accessories are from Bamboula, Ltd.; and the textile is from Indigo Arts.** RIGHT: **Striking color, bold images, and curvaceous form characterize this hall display. Three dazzling Haitian vodoo flags covered in sequins add shimmer to this colorful space. The largest, La Siren, was created by Haitian artist Wagler Vital. Lush delphiniums, a wire-crafted cage, a silver tray with African beads, and other items rest on an African-inspired table design by Cheryl Levin and Bob Phillips. Wall hangings are from Indigo Arts.**

Display Essentials

In many parts of Africa, corner stores are nonexistent and restaurants unheard of. People often make everything for their homes—food, clothing, furnishings. They collect various treasures and mementos, and show them off with pride. This sets African-style design apart from other interior decorating styles. Accessorizing in African style means working with the things you already have and giving them a new, African life. It means displaying those little things you take pride in and value. Although a certain amount of clutter can

ABOVE: Wood sculptured figurines from the Ivory Coast, a framed snippet of Kente cloth, small ceramics, and a lamp and vase from the 1950s reflect a more stylized approach to collecting. This assemblage obviously takes its cue from the overall feel of the room.
RIGHT: A small space in a Philadelphia loft apartment has been transformed into a cozy bedroom. The bed is covered in a hand-batik Adire quilt design, produced by Nigerian textile artist Adeshola Olaniyi. The quilt is available at LSF for Wonoo Ventures, Ltd. The pillow cases are covered in silk, the decorative standing screen is covered in tightly woven burlap with silk ribbon arranged in a geometric pattern, and the ceramic bowl is designed by Joan Harrington.

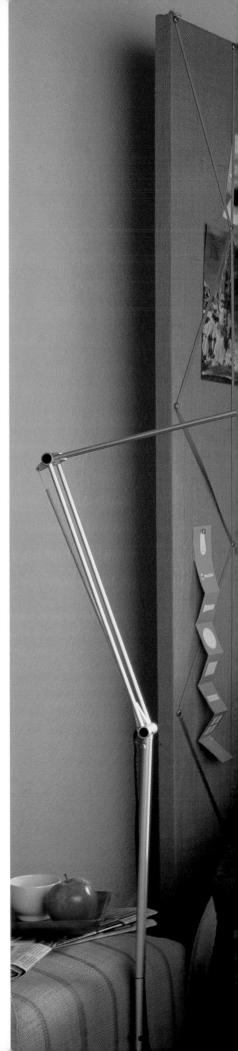

create a cozy atmosphere, beware of its pitfalls—that claustrophobic crush of objects, however well loved. Keep in mind the collector's creed: the only things worth having are the things you *really* love. A few display guidelines can help you show off your accessories to their best effect.

HARMONY

Color, texture, form, and proportion are at their best when they are in harmony. Avoid too much of a good thing. Instead, strike a balance between disparate elements. Tall ceramic pots, round plates on stands, flat baskets—different shapes, sizes, and levels make for an interesting display. Keep the same principle in mind when it comes to color and texture. Bold patterns balance out smaller prints, and vibrant colors mix well with softer hues. You can work interesting African textiles into your design scheme as pillows, cushions, or throws. Creating a harmonious display is much like putting together the pieces of a jigsaw puzzle. Don't be afraid to mix traditional African accessories with contemporary, modern, or even industrial elements. African style is all about such eclectic combinations. In the wise words of a friend of mine: "It is a feeling. You can't define and embrace Africa. Africa embraces you and all that is yours."

GROUPING

Tell a story with your collections by grouping them in a meaningful way. Blending your objects together into a united whole requires that they have something in common— the same frame, the same theme, or the same color. Most visual artists will tell you that three is the magic number of display. Whether the configuration is horizontal or vertical, the trinity configuration attracts the gaze. If you have many pieces to arrange in a single group, try to create one large shape with the objects.

Grouping pictures and photographs makes a stronger visual impact than placing them randomly around the room. Let the perimeter of the frames create a pleasing shape. Place the pictures on the floor and try different combinations before you start

OPPOSITE: The focal point of this mantel is Dressler Smith's signature painting, "Egyptian Water Lilies." Symmetry is created by positioning three terra-cotta potted plants to its left and antique wood pins and Ghanaian colonial figures to the right, which in turn lends formality to the mantel. Color, texture, form, and proportion are best when in balance. A mix of vertical and horizontal, short and tall, flat and three-dimensional shapes gives a collection greater interest.

to pound nails into your walls. Be mindful of the distance between the works, and hang the pictures at a viewing height of approximately 5 feet 6 inches from the floor. Hallways are the perfect place for hanging; corridor walls can give a gallery feel to displays of photographs, mirrors, small wall hangings, or pictures.

Some words of caution to those thinking of hanging older, delicate, or colorful textiles: Make sure that you protect them from direct sunlight, and if you begin to notice any discoloration, take the textile down from the wall. Framing older textiles is an option. Placing delicate pieces behind glass will preserve them for years to come. But many are reluctant to frame their textiles. After all, an essential part of their beauty is their handmade, tactile quality, which can be lost under glass.

Grouping is also critical for pottery, figurines, and baskets. Living rooms, libraries, and corridors are great places to show off your collections. Fireplaces, bookcases, coffee tables, and end tables are perfect spots for grouping accessories. Or leave the doors of an armoire or cabinet open and show off your folded textiles, dolls, musical instruments, or jewelry.

Accessories may be small things, but they are the final touches that have the power to make a big impact when they are artfully arranged. Delightful to the eye, sumptuous to the touch, they are a rich and personal way to express who you are and to transform a house into a home. So select accessories you love, display them with care, and let them tell your story and the story of Africa.

LEFT: Rarely do we take the time to celebrate our past and those who have paved the way for us. Karen Dugger has found space in a deep windowsill where she displays photos of several generations of her relatives, from a great grandfather who served in World War I to her daughter. OPPOSITE: A simple collection of treasured belongings on a bedside table forms a personal still life. Made of serpentine stone, a Shona sculpture of a woman with traditional coiffure sits atop a collection of nighttime reading. The Liz Galbraith lamp, while not African inspired, captures the organic quality of African style. The Shona sculpture is from Pearl of Africa.

before

Fireplace mantelpieces are perfect places to show off your accessories. A conventional collection of glass, porcelain, copper frames and an antique box make an attractive but not very lively mantel display. African art, however, is so expressive that it always lends itself to uniquely beautiful arrangements. Look at the spark when we accessorize with a mix of African and Haitian artwork. From left to right: an East African vessel, a metal sculpture of a Dogon horseman, a Haitian steel drum sculpture by Gabriel Bien-Aimé mounted on the wall, an assortment of boxes, several Kenyan spearheads, and a Nigerian wood sculpture placed in front of a basket from Kenya.

after

Burlap-Covered Standing Screen

This burlap-covered standing screen with a design made from ribbon and upholstery tacks is not just a functional piece of furniture. You can also use it as a display board for your favorite photographs or for whatever little accessories touch your spirit.

Materials

Three hollow-core doors 18 inches wide and of standard height

Enough burlap or fabric of your choice to cover all three doors, front and back

Staple gun

Spool of heavy ribbon

Decorative upholstery tacks

Scissors

Hinges

simple way in which these elements come together in a harmonious whole.

Interior decorating can be extremely intimidating for many people. Basic rules of design can guide us, but the greatest secret of design is that there is no one way to decorate. If you want a truly creative interior, you'll have to adopt a more individualized approach. Don't be concerned with matching like with like; that usually produces a one-size-fits-all look. Instead, think about the mix: decorate with shapes, lines, colors, and textures that speak to you, even if they come from different design eras. Create a unique take on African style by incorporating elements of other design styles into your own African vision.

The mix means not settling for the obvious. As in life, so in design: Never underestimate the element of surprise. By combining rough and refined, light and dark, vintage and new, organic and synthetic—we invite unexpected beauty into our homes. Above all, trust your judgment and you won't go wrong. African style is one of the few design styles that is simply too diverse to be codified into a standard look. So let your own sense of style be your guide to capturing the spirit of Africa.

PREVIOUS PAGES: Curvaceous, sophisticated, and classic, this sculptural black leather butterfly chair and 1950s free-form floor lamp share the African quality of progressive simplicity. RIGHT: The door panels of this uniquely designed armoire and entertainment unit, made of solid cherry and basswood, were inspired by the patterns found in Ghanaian Kente cloth. This is designed by Richard L. Bryant for International Design Group.

African Country

The word "country" summons up images of open campfires, hooked rugs, handmade quilts, rustic pottery, and big weathered tables. And country style is steeped in nostalgia; it is a gesture toward the past, an attempt to recapture in our homes times gone by. African Country is at once pastoral and adventurous, rugged and cozy, traditional and sophisticated. It evokes the savanna plains of East Africa—the Sudan, Kenya, and Tanzania—rough country, where many inhabitants are still connected to the land and pull up stakes four or five times a year as they follow their herds' seasonal migration.

Furniture plays a major role in creating the East African Country look. Leather, wood, wicker, rope, cane, and other durable materials have the rugged natural elegance that is the key to this style. Choose sofas and chairs that are comfortable and casual. Wood, leather, metal, and fiber details will add warmth to your interior. Make sure you lay your hands on an East African stool as well. The simple design of such stools blends beautifully in country-style interiors. Masks are not extensively produced in this region of the continent. If you do decide to include them, make sure they don't compete with East African accessories such as trays, boxes, baskets, carpets, walking sticks, spears, beaded necklaces, and bags.

Incorporate earth colors into your East African Country interior—hues such as rust, ocher, beige, and terra-cotta,

OPPOSITE: This selection of furnishings exudes the feel of East Africa cattle country in varying tones of browns, ranging from coffee and pecan to cinnamon and sand. Wood, leather, metals, clay, silver, cottons, linens, and sisal—what a wonderful balance of African textures and tones. The armoire and mirror are designed by Richard Bryant. The sofa and armchair are designed by Allan Price. All pieces are available at Kente Ventures, Inc. The Tiv lounge chair is available at Indigo Arts.

Making the Screen

1. Staple fabric at center of door. Stretch fabric across the front and around the back until the fabric meets. Staple fabric at the back.
2. Make your design with the ribbon and tacks.
3. Repeat steps 1 and 2 for the next two panels. Make sure that you position the fabric so that the pattern will line up evenly on all three doors.
4. Hinge doors 1 and 2 together so that they fold flat when face-to-face.
5. Hinge doors 2 and 3 together so that they fold flat back-to-back.

The Mix

Over the years, I have collected a number of photographs of beautiful rooms. Covering the walls of my office, they lift my spirits as a fine painting might. Some rooms appeal to me because of their tranquil colors, others because of their unusual fabrics and finishes. But, more generally, I chose to display these rooms because of the relaxed and

which evoke a rural connection to Mother Nature—by opting for casually sophisticated linen, canvas, raw silk, and other textured fabrics. Keep your walls light in contrast to the wooden furnishings and fabrics: soft yellows and neutral tones work well. Complete your East African Country look with rustic finishes such as wrought iron, copper, silver, reed, and sisal, which you can find in such accessories as shields, spears, trays, and beadwork.

The country look is not restricted to East Africa. If you prefer bright colors, look to West Africa for baskets, gourds, pottery, masks, figurines, and pillows made of woven Ewe cloth. And make sure you take advantage of the region's rich weaving tradition: Wall hangings, bedspreads, and other textiles are central to the West African Country look. For a more familiar country feeling, combine these African-inspired elements with such American staples as patchwork quilts and twig furniture and paintings.

Classical Africa

This classical look is sophisticated and expresses Africa in a traditional way. Rooms feel more formal, with furniture arrangements that are symmetrical and balanced. The higher quality of furnishings is obvious at a glance. Here you can use lots of art and accessories; textiles should be carefully coordinated. Aesthetically and functionally, this classical style unmistakably defines a room as African.

Sofas and chairs with frames of dark tropical woods enhance this feeling as do fabrics inspired by traditional patterns. Luxurious African textiles like Kente and Ewe cloths, once they are machine-reinforced and stain treated, become perfect upholstery choices for chairs and ottomans. In addition, animal prints for ottomans and other accent furnishings, as well as soft wool patterned carpets, enhance this look. To tie this sumptuous look together, use wall colors that are rich and reflect Africa's vast diversity of cultures and ecology.

OPPOSITE: Ethiopian hand-carved chairs are unique within African design, where stools are more common. Their chair backs are often carved with open geometric design, seats are scooped out in bowl-like forms, and the base support traditionally has a three-legged support. Another unique piece is this body mask from Kenya, worn during ceremonies by men when their wives are pregnant. While the specific ritual meaning is varied, some say it is worn to show support for the women. The exquisite design and craftsmanship do indeed appear to be a loving homage to mother and child. The Ethiopian chair is from Craft Caravan. The body mask is from a private collection of the East Africa Resource and Study Center.

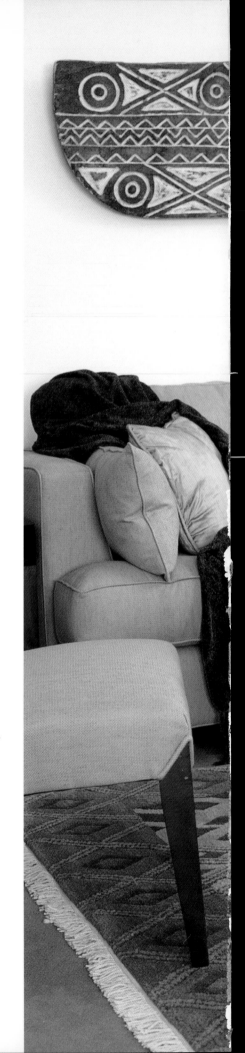

Function should be a priority in every interior, but classical African interiors focus on art and design. Travelers and collectors will find comfort in this classical style, which allows for everything to have its place. Sculpture, masks, figurines, and other art objects become the focus of a room when they are displayed as a collection. For your displays, you can choose glass-door cabinets, mount objects on a wall, or place them on a beautiful wood-grain table. Even the smallest collectibles, such as brass boxes, ceramics, jewelry, or coins, become treasures when they are lovingly displayed. This is a style that goes to the heart of Africa.

Afro-Euro

Afro-Euro combines African style and Art Deco. The early modern style of the 1920s and 1930s accentuates the exotic elegance and modern simplicity of African art and design. Art Deco evokes the spirited music of the jazz age, the popularity of African and Cubist art, and the glamour of Hollywood's heyday.

Creating an early modern feel in our homes requires a healthy passion for antique shops, flea markets, and auctions. Here will you find affordable treasures from the Art Deco period, furniture that exudes luxury and grace. Sofas from this period vary in form: Some have streamlined rounded bodies with gracefully curved arms; others have rigid, tailored

RIGHT: A mixture of African pattern design and the tailored lines and contrasting textures of French Art Deco gives this interior its distinctly Afro-Euro flavor. The use of quiet, calming neutrals allows African patterns to be subtly introduced into the design scheme. Earthbound colors, characteristic of African style, are found in the pillows upholstered in two different raffia-woven textiles, an enormous butterfly mask adorned with geometric symbols, an African-inspired hand-woven area carpet and a rolled-arm chaise. The chaise is designed by Larry Laslo; the sofa and chairs are from Directional, available at The Menagerie, Ltd.; and the rug is from Tufenkian Tibetan Carpets.

backs and chunky feet. The simple club chairs of the 1920s fit beautifully into African-style interiors. Look for pieces that are low and wide, upholstered in leather or sumptuous textured fabrics. You can also opt for more affordable reproductions of Art Deco furnishings; most lack the fine details of the originals, but their basic design is still quite beautiful. And make sure that you invest in a few works of African art. It looks simply stunning silhouetted against an Art Deco backdrop. The basic shapes and forms of the region's art chime with the clean lines of the period's tailored furnishings.

LEFT: The bold imagery of Africa mixes comfortably with the neoclassic and early-modern furnishings collected by designers Cheryl Campbell and David Teague. Framed by a pair of lamps designed by David Teague, an oversized sofa claims center stage of this Afro-Euro interior. On the coffee table rest a Fang mask from Gabon, ostrich eggs, and other items. A Senufo stool adds a distinctively African presence, as do spears from Kenya and a wooden decorative tent stake from Morocco. Teague was inspired by French and American designers when he modified a 1930 French iron gate to make the contemporary coffee table. The furniture is available at America Antiques & Design; the artifacts are from Indigo Arts; the Moroccan tent stake is available at Beads of Paradise; and the stools are from Craft Caravan. ABOVE: A chaise upholstered in faux-zebra fabric, a Brancusi-like wire drum table, an Art Deco–inspired armchair and geometric Kente-like symbols in the carpet create an eclectic Afro-Euro mix. The furnishings are available at The Menagerie, Ltd. The carpet is designed by Barbara Barry and is available at Tufenkian Tibetan Carpets.

The colors that best capture this period fall into two families: neutral tones, creamy beiges, and soft whites; and muted sages, mustards, and plums. Pattern will enhance the look. You can opt for geometric patterns such as the Egyptian sunrise motif or stylized crescents, which were popular during the 1920s and 1930s. Or choose African motifs and patterns in more neutral tones, especially Kubas, Showas, and other textiles made from raffia and rough fibers. Fabric inspired by the African cheetah and zebra; finishes such as rosewood and mahogany, mother-of-pearl and decorative inlays—all link the spirit of Africa to an early modern attitude.

Afro Retro

Afro Retro mixes African style with midcentury modern furniture. A blend of influences—abstract art, African design, and functionalism—produced pieces that are now classics of design. Harry Bertoia's diamond chair, Charles Eames's plywood chair, and Finn Juhl's chieftain chair are just a few quintessential examples. Like African stools, furnishings of the 1940s and 1950s are akin to functional works of art.

Something about the asymmetrical, graphic form of 1950s porcelain and of amoeba-shaped coffee tables with tapered legs harmonizes with the organic design of a Senufo carved wooden bed or with the abstract style of Kota reliquary figures from Gabon. A simple leather butterfly chair and floor lamp can be the perfect partners for an Ethiopian stool or

RIGHT: **What better way to preserve fond memories than to surround yourself with the things you love: The Baumanns' collection of baskets, pottery, and figurines are mostly from East Africa. A casual assemblage of furniture completes the mix, including a woven leather chair from Kenya, a red leather contemporary African stool, and a butterfly chair next to a three-legged Ethiopian stool. This room is unmistakably the home of travelers and collectors.**

textile. Often upholstered in leather and wool, furniture from the 1940s and 1950s is always comfortable and easy to integrate into African-style interiors. You might want to choose a sofa that wraps around a room, and complement it with lamps and other accessories that are organic in form. Make sure you include an African stool or two to

ABOVE: Kuba, Asoke, and mud cloth are at home here. The cushions of this vintage IKEA sofa are reupholstered in mud cloth; the stacking tables, end table, and table lamp are all flea market finds. The Dogan chair from Mali and Diamond chair by Harry Bertoia are both classics. Draped textiles available at Beads of Paradise. On the rear wall is a handpainted relief print, "Les Oiseaux au Jardin d'Or," by artist Nefertiti.

highlight the sculpted quality of the period's furnishings. You can look to Cara Greenberg's *Mid-Century Modern,* among many other books on the furniture style of the period, as a resource for images and ideas.

Many of the pieces from the 1940s and 1950s are airy and lightweight; their beauty lies in their lines and form. Graceful furniture like this demands softer-colored walls as a backdrop to take full advantage of its forms. But because of the furniture's unusual, almost quirky design, you can also afford to have fun. Display bold and graphic African textiles as wall hangings or drape them over furnishings. Avoid extremely vibrant colors. Choose, for instance, Ewe cloths in muted primary colors such as burnt orange or lime green, or long strips of Kuba cloth in contrasting creams and browns. Mud cloth in all colors also mixes well with this furniture. Window treatments should be light and soft, sheer enough to allow sunlight in so that lovely shadows are cast over the beautiful forms. Sisal or wool carpets in muted colors add to the organic feel of the interior and contrast well with the bases of the furniture. Keep African and early modern accessories to simple forms. In a minimal interior such as this, subtlety speaks volumes.

Planning and designing a beautiful home for the way we truly live—a home that fills us with joy, creates a sense of meaning, and exudes an aura of calm—is a pretty tall order, particularly in today's hectic world. I can recall my mother announcing the five major furniture styles of her day: Italian Provincial, French Provincial, Mediterranean, Early American, Danish Modern. Decorating then was as simple as taking your pick. But the world has changed, and today we look to our homes for more than just a series of pretty rooms. We search for a place of calm that speaks of our past and grows with us as we move toward the future.

African style, the reflection of an age-old continent, can fill our homes with the aesthetic and spiritual qualities we desire, and at the same time fulfill our functional needs. Organic colors that soothe and comfort, symbolic patterns and designs, stools, textiles—Africa offers us traditions that celebrate the home, family, and history. Creating a home in African style means summoning up and extending ourselves into the very space we live in. It means invoking the rich spirit of Africa, down to the details.

resources

Furniture

Anthropologie
201 West Lancaster Avenue
Wayne, Pennsylvania 19087
610-687-4141
Tunisian sea grass chair and imported home furnishings.

Ashanti Origins
202-857-9705
www.ashantiorigins.com
Contemporary African furniture and accessories.

Baker Furniture
1661 Monroe Avenue, NW
Grand Rapids, Michigan 49505
1-800-59-BAKER
Finn Juhl Collection and a wide selection of period styles.

Cob Web
440 Lafayette Street
New York, New York 10012
212-505-1558
Moroccan furniture and wrought-iron furnishings.

J. Camp Designs
11 Longford Street
Philadelphia, Pennsylvania 19136
215-333-9060
Sculptural wood furniture, specializing in walnut slab tables.

Kente Ventures, Inc.
Contact: Inside Design Ltd.
1245 Medary Avenue
Philadelphia, Pennsylvania 19141
Sharne@Insidedesignltd.com
Authentic African-inspired furniture, accessories, and African textiles for upholstery.

Lamu Industries
1 Fifth Avenue
New York, New York 10003
212-473-8591
www.lamu.com
Hand-carved mahogany tables from Lamu, Kenya.

The Menagerie, Ltd.
2400 Market Street
Philadelphia, Pennsylvania 19103
215-561-5041
Period and contemporary home furnishings and accessories.

Padouk Design
Epee Ellong
New York, New York
718-399-1995
www.Padoukdesign.com
Specializing in contemporary African ottomans, stools, and accent furnishings.

Phillips Metal
131 Upland Terrace
Bala Cynwyd, Pennsylvania 19004
610-664-1436; fax: 610-668-7758
Wrought-iron and hand-painted ethnic and African-inspired furniture.

Period Furniture

America Antiques & Design
5 South Main Street
Lambertville, New Jersey 08530
609-397-6966
www.Americadesigns.com.
American and French nineteenth- and twentieth-century antiques.

Barry Dwaine Burton
Blacksmith & Welder
Philadelphia, Pennsylvania
215-844-0834
Custom-made chairs and tables from vintage wrought iron.

Cape Island Collectibles
Sea Horse Antiques
Route 109 & Second Avenue
Cape May, New Jersey 08024
609-886-5998
Mid-century modern furniture and African art.

Findings
246 Race Street
Philadelphia, Pennsylvania 19106
215-923-0988
Antiques, reproductions, collectibles, and African art.

Jacksons 20th-Century Design
Tyska Brinken 20
11127 Stockholm, Sweden
468 411 85 87
Mid-century and early modern designs.

Lumier
112 North Third Street
Philadelphia, Pennsylvania 19106
215-922-6908
Mid-century furniture and accessories.

Malmaison Antiques
253 East 47th Street
New York, New York 10021
212-288-7569
Egyptian revival, empire furniture, and African art.

Mode Moderne
North Third Street
Philadelphia, Pennsylvania 19106
215-627-0299
Mid-century and early modern classic furnishings.

Home Accessories

Adela's Functional Art
830-13 A1A North, Suite 142
Ponte Vedra Beach, Florida 32082
904-273-7453
Decorative knobs, handles, and switch plates.

Bamboula, Ltd.
164 West Walnut Street
Kutztown, Pennsylvania 19530
610-894-4800, 610-894-9737
Contemporary African art and craft for the home.

Blackberry at Macy's
Herald Square at 34th Street
New York, New York 10001
212-494-3751, 703-418-1506
African furniture, table accessories, and home furnishings.

Garden Traditions
131 Heller Way
Montclair, New Jersey 07043
973-509-1996
Traditional and contemporary African pots and garden accessories.

Harris, the Rarest SwitchPlate
3008 Albion Road
Cleveland, Ohio 44120
216-295-8644
Decorative switch plates.

Hermes
41 Madison Avenue
New York, New York 10010
212-751-3181
The "Africa" tableware series and other fine china.

Home Zone
56 North Third Street
Philadelphia, Pennsylvania 19106
215-592-4215
Eclectic mix of home accessories.

Houles U.S.A.
8584 Melrose Avenue
Los Angeles, California 90069
310-652-6171
Fabric, trimmings, and decorative accessories

IKEA Inc.
Customer Service Center
800-434-IKEA (4532)
Contemporary furniture and home accessories.

Merit Ventures
244 Madison Avenue, Suite 343
New York, New York 10016
800-631-7241, 212-840-9899
Decorative boxes and trays.

Serengeti Plains
615 Bloomfield Avenue
Montclair, New Jersey 07042
973-783-2883, 973-783-2828
www.serengetiplains.com
African-inspired home furnishings.

Tribal Links
267 South Stone, Studio F
Tucson, Arizona 85701
520-623-8654
www.tribalinks.com
Traditional African art and crafts, jewelry, and furniture.

African Galleries and Studios

Beads of Paradise
16 East 17th Street
New York, New York 10003
212-620-0642
Beads, semi-precious stones, traditional African textiles, and art objects.

Bomani Gallery
251 Post Street
San Francisco, California 94108
415-296-8677
International fine arts.

Craft Caravan
63 Greene Street
New York, New York 10012
212-431-6669
Traditional African textiles, stools, jewelry, and art objects.

Gallery Alina
P.O. Box 5013
Framingham, Massachusetts 01701
617-261-6060, ext. 18
www.artzimbabwe.com
Contemporary decorative and fine art from Southern Africa.

Haneef's Bookstore and Mosi
911 Orange Street
Wilmington, Delaware 19801
302-656-4193
Hanefbkst1@aol.com
Books, gifts, and accessories.

Indigo Arts
153 North Third Street
Philadelphia, Pennsylvania 29206
215-922-4041
www.indigoarts.com
African and ethnic textiles, furniture, and decorative accents.

Oyo Gallery for Traditional African Art
573 Bloomfield Avenue
Montclair, New Jersey 07042
973-509-7555
Olanre@aol.com
Traditional and tribal art.

Pearl of Africa
732 South Street
Philadelphia, Pennsylvania 19147
215-413-8995
African art and cultural items.

Sisters Space and Books
1515 U Street, NW
Washington, D.C. 20009
202-332-3433
Books by and about African-American women, jewelry, and personal gifts.

Timbuktu
408 East 13th Street
New York, New York 10009
212-473-4955
Moroccan home furnishings and accessories.

Unan Imports
6971 North Sheridan Road
Chicago, Illinois 60626
773-274-4022
Traditional African sculpture, textile, basketry, and jewelry.

Zawadi
1524 U Street NW
Washington, DC 20009
African home accessories, textiles, art, and gifts.

Resource Information

Aid to Artisans
14 Brick Lane
Farmington, Connecticut 06032
860-677-1649
International craft organization, providing assistance to artists worldwide.

East Africa Resource and Study Center
407 North 33rd Street
Philadelphia, Pennsylvania 19104
215-382-3191
Education outreach specializing in nomadic peoples of East Africa.

Images of the Motherland
P.O. Box 1017
Philadelphia, Pennsylvania 19105
215-848-3651
www.imagesofthemotherland.com
Live performances and resources for Dogan art and design.

Carpets and Floor Coverings

J. P. Wilborg
Sibyllegatan 35 & 41
11442 Stockholm, Sweden
8 783 0265
International selection of antique carpets and rare African art.

Material Culture
4700 Wissahickon Avenue, No. 101
Philadelphia, Pennsylvania 19144
215-849-8030
International assortment of ethnic-style carpets and accessories.

Pottery Barn
3250 Van Ness Avenue
San Francisco, California 94109
415-421-7900
Sea grass and sisal area carpet.

Tufenkian Tibetan Carpets
902 Broadway, 2nd floor
New York, New York 10010-6002
212-475-2475
Contemporary African-inspired primitive chic collection.

Textiles

A & J Fabrics
752 South Fourth Street
Philadelphia, Pennsylvania 19147
215-592-7011
Traditional and contemporary textiles and cloths.

Arte Wallcovering and Fabrics, Inc.
16578 West Park Circle Drive
Chagrin Falls, Ohio 44023-4550
800-338-ARTE, 800-775-0609, 440-543-0366
African-inspired upholstery fabrics and wallpapers.

B.I.T.H.
9 Hector Avenue
Toronto, Canada M6G 3G2
416-588-6751
African-inspired table and bed linens, pillows, and other accents.

Country Elegance
269 South 20th Street
Philadelphia, Pennsylvania 19103
215-545-2992
Fine bed and table linens.

Djema Imports
70 West 125 Street
New York, New York 10027-4429
212-289-3842
www.djemaimports.com
Wide selection of African textiles.

Handmasters
Handmasters Studio
Tihera Amatallah
5555 Germantown Avenue
Philadelphia, Pennsylvania 19144
Traditional and contemporary African textiles.

LSF for Wonoo Ventures, Ltd.
1657 The Fairway, Suite 150
Jenkintown, Pennsylvania 19046
215-782-8489
Authentic Kente and African stools.

Michael's Upholstery
615 South Sixth Street
Philadelphia, Pennsylvania 19147
215-592-0256, 215-474-1928
Upholstering antique furniture.

Quilters of the Round Table
5038 Hazel Avenue
Philadelphia, Pennsylvania 19143
215-748-5022
African-American quilts and wall hangings.

Sew Simple & So Unique
Marion Merriweather
P.O. Box 44233
Indianapolis, Indiana 46244-0233
317-578-5462
African-inspired pillows and cushions.

Visual Feast Fabrics
Dan Sekanwagi
P.O. Box 441811
Houston, Texas 77244-1811
281-530-6585
members.aol.com/visualfeast
Contemporary African upholstery textiles.

Lighting

Galbraith and Paul
307 North Third Street
Philadelphia, Pennsylvania 19106
215-923-4632
Lampshades of handmade papers, pillows, and quilts.

Lee's Studio
Marketplace Design Center
Philadelphia, Pennsylvania 19103
215-568-7000
Modern, contemporary, and designer lighting.

Visions by Marie
Nives Marie Pere
1106 West 70th Street
Los Angeles, California 90044
323-778-1677
Lamps and other accessories covered in African cloth.

Artists

Inside Design, Ltd.
Sharne Algotsson
1245 Medary Avenue
Philadelphia, Pennsylvania 19141
Sharne@Insidedesignltd.com
www.insidedesignltd.com
Interior design, styling, and event decoration.

Cheryl Levin
Bala Cynwyd, Pennsylvania
610-664-1436
Faux painting and other decorative wall and furniture painting.

Nefertiti
Montclair, New Jersey
973-783-0907, 973-509-1693
Relief prints and paintings.

Wendy Osterweil
Philadelphia, Pennsylvania
215-849-8768
Linocut prints and fiber art.

Janet Taylor Pickett
Montclair, New Jersey
973-429-1620, 973-744-6354
pickett@email.njin.net
Artwork on paper, pastels, and collage.

Jim Powell
129 East Ash Street
Jackson, Mississippi 39202
601-352-7248
Interior and afrocentric garden design.

Sister Dolls
Ingrid Andrews
1375 Matinal Circle
San Diego, California 92127
619-674-6258
African-American handmade cloth dolls.

Dressler Smith
P.O. Box 1182
Belmar, New Jersey 08099-5182
609-728-5825
Paintings to touch the spirit, pastels, and oils.

Uptown Tribal
Adrienne L. Lockett
East Orange, New Jersey 07018
973-673-2375
Amber and silver African-inspired jewelry and hand-made books and accessories.

Paints and Supplies

Home Depot
800-553-3199
www.Homedepot.com
Wall paints and supplies.

Pearl Art and Craft Supplies, Inc.
417 South Street
Philadelphia, Pennsylvania 19147
215-238-1900
Decorative paint, glazes, varnish, brushes, and equipment.

bibliography

Adler, Peter, and Nicholas Barnard. *Asafo!: African Flags of the Fante*. London: Thames and Hudson Ltd., 1992.

Algotsson, Sharne, and Denys Davis. *The Spirit of African Design*. New York: Clarkson N. Potter, 1996.

Changuion, Paul. *The African Mural*. London: New Holland, 1989.

Courtney-Clarke, Margaret. *African Canvas: The Art of West African Women*. New York: Rizzoli International, 1990.

Fiell, Charlotte, and Peter Fiell. *1000 Chairs*. Koln: Taschen, 1997.

Garner, Phillippe. *Twentieth Century Furniture*. New York: Van Nostrand Rheinhold, 1980.

Greenberg, Cara, and Tim Street-Porter. *Mid-Century Modern: Furniture of the 1950s*. New York: Harmony Books, 1984.

Ketchum, William C., Jr. *Furniture 2: Neoclassic to the Present*. New York: Cooper-Hewitt Museum, 1981.

Kirkham, Pat, and Charles and Ray Eames. *Designers of the Twentieth Century*. Massachusetts: The MIT Press, 1995.

Lakin, Dennis. *Kenya, Nature's Bounty*. Chicago: Passport Books, 1992.

Massey, Anne. *Interior Design of the 20th Century*. London: Thames and Hudson, 1990.

Maybury-Lewis, David. *Millennium: Tribal Wisdom & the Modern World*. New York: Viking Penguin, 1992.

National Museum of African Art. *History, Design, and Craft in West African Strip-Woven Cloth*. United States of America: Smithsonian Institution, 1992.

National Museum of African Art. "Elmina, Art and Trade on the West African Coast." Washington, D.C.: Smithsonian Institution, 1992–1993.

Picton, John and John Mack. *African Textiles*. London: British Museum Publications, 1989.

Polakoff, Claire. *Into Indigo: African Textiles and Dyeing Techniques*. London: Routledge and Kegan Paul, 1982.

Robbins, Warren M., and Nancy Ingram Nooter. *African Art in American Collections: Survey 1989*. Washington/London: Smithsonian Press, 1989.

Rybczynski, Witold. *Home: A Short History of an Idea*. New York: Penguin Books, 1987.

Willborg, Peter. *Textiles from Five Centuries*. Stockholm: J. P. Willborg Publications, 1995.

index